High Priestess

By the same author

The Witches Speak
Witch Blood!
The Secrets of Ancient Witchcraft
Witchcraft in Yorkshire
Lid Off the Cauldron
Witches Were for Hanging
The Zodiac Experience

This book is published in England as *One Witch's World*

High Priestess

The Life & Times of Patricia Crowther

Patricia Crowther

Phoenix Publishing

PHOENIX PUBLISHING, INC.
P.O. Box 3829
Blaine, Washington USA 98231
www.phoenixpublishing.com

Published in the U.K. by
ROBERT HALE LTD.
45-47 Clerkenwell Green
London EC1R 0HT

ISBN 0-919345-87-5

Cover design by Creative Circus

Printed in the U.S.A.

Contents

To Ian – for his understanding and
indefatigable patience during the
production of this book

Acknowledgements

I wish to thank Rider (Random House UK Limited) for permission to quote from *Witchcraft Today* by Gerald B. Gardner; Faber & Faber to quote Lawrence Durrell's superb description of 'Aphrodite Thalassia' from his *Reflections on a Marine Venus*; The Society of the Inner Light to quote from *Through the Gates of Death* by Dion Fortune; Howard Rodway for words from his book, *Tarot of the Old Path*; Taina Ketola for her telling thoughts from *The New Astrology*; and (the Executors of) the late W. Walter Gill to quote extracts from *A Second Manx Scrapbook*.

My thanks are also extended to Chris Selwood for nostalgic and amusing letters about Fiveacres Sun Club at St Albans; Alan Wharton for his loyalty and honour; Jim Davies of Ontario for interesting information, and Eleanor (Ray) Bone for a long-standing friendship.

I am also indebted to Mark S. Graham, creator of *The Original Ghost Walk* in York, for prompting my memory of Harry Martindale's ghostly encounter; Geoff Smith for the quote from *Knights of the Solar Cross*, and the *Bournemouth Daily Echo* for permission to quote from an article they featured on 25 February 1986.

Illustrations 5 and 7 are by courtesy of the *Daily Express* and the *Yorkshire Post* respectively.

List of Illustrations

Credits

Daily Express: 5. *Yorkshire Post*: 7. Ian Lilleyman: 9. Eileen Smith: 10. Christ Selwood: 12. J. Edward Vickers OBE: 13. Kathy Billington: 15.

All other photographs are from the author's collection.

1 Myself when Young

My mother, Clare Dawson, was like hundreds of other mothers who, notwithstanding the advice of Sir Noel Coward's famous song, wanted their daughters to go 'on the stage'. I was a very timid and shy child and, when taken out of the home environment, cried a lot. This may have been due to my mother's fears of being seen heavily pregnant (she always went for walks at night, despite being a respectable married lady at the time). She was a good-looking, vivacious person – a lordly Leo, who always dressed in the height of fashion – so her aversion could have been due to pride of appearance. The pianist at a hotel in Brighton once wrote a vaguely acrostic verse to her:

> Knives are made in her native town;
> Let them never cut friendship true.
> And may her hair, so golden brown,
> Reflect her spirit's warmth anew.
>
> Dancer elite – and yet so cool,
> Artistic in her mode of dress.
> Wifely in conduct, spurning rule,
> Sympathy sharing, none the less.
>
> On her bright head may the Sun e'er shine,
> Nascent with thoughts that are sublime.

Mother's labour was prolonged for three days, and the doctor said that she had had enough pains to bring three babies into the world. (He was an excellent doctor by all accounts and finally gave her something called a 'black draught', presumably a knock-out drug.) The nurse who was present at the birth said the doctor had a tough time, not to mention my mother! It was a dry birth, and I got stuck in the birth-canal, so he had to deliver me with forceps (it may be difficult to believe, but I definitely remember being dragged from that warm, watery place, and the pain from those forceps clamped to my tiny head). The doctor muttered, 'It's too late for the child. I'll save the mother.' However, knowing how much my mother wanted me, the nurse gave me a few good slaps and I started to breathe for myself. I had made it!

I was born at 12.30 a.m. in the middle of a thunderstorm when the Moon was waning. The Sun stood in the sign of Libra, and Leo claimed ascendancy of my birth-chart.

Apart from the harrowing experience of being born, my earliest recollections include lying in my lavender satin and cream lace cot; being at my mother's breast, and falling off my father's knee! I also recall sitting in my high-chair at the table and being instructed to copy my parents' actions so as to learn the proper use of cutlery.

I can clearly see my paternal grandmother, Elizabeth, or 'Tizzy', in my mind's eye, even though I was only two years old when she died. She was a petite, gentle old lady, and I remember sitting upon her knee. She always wore a fox-fur cape with a posy of fresh violets pinned to it, and I would stroke the soft fur and press my face against the sweet-smelling flowers. Her maiden name had been Machin, which means 'fairy' or 'elf', and one wonders whether she was descended from the fairy people, those tiny human beings who lived in ages past. These fairy people are not to be confused with story-book fairies, nor even with Ken Dodd's 'Diddy Men'! Long ago in the Isle of Man there was the 'Battle of Fairy Bridge', when the little people took on the giants, or anyone over five feet in height! In Sheffield there is a place called Machin Bank, or Fairy Bank, although 'giants' live there, now!

A fortune-teller, one Madame Melba, lived next door to us, and her window displayed a picture of a large hand showing the palm's various lines. (This lady had a son whose nickname was 'Jumpy' – although I never discovered why he merited it. However, many years later I received a letter from 'Jumpy' which revealed he had settled in the States and that his profession was dentistry. I wondered if his mother had foreseen his future occupation and if that had been the reason for his nickname!) Madame Melba told my parents that I would become well known in the future, and that the Moon's influence would be strong in my life, bestowing the gift of 'clear sight'. She also gave me a small crystal bowl, announcing that the chalice stood for protection; whether this referred to her gift or to something more mystical was unclear, but my parents thanked her and Mother nodded her head gravely (she never scoffed at anything connected with psychic matters).

My parents were members of the Builders Exchange, a private businessmen's club which often held fancy-dress dances. On one occasion my mother went as 'Night' and won first prize. (Arrayed in an exquisite gown of black voile spangled with stars and deep-blue jewels, set off by a crescent-moon headdress, she could easily have represented the 'Goddess of the Moon'). At this club's Christmas party, I and other children were dressed as fairies, but I was chosen to be the 'Fairy on the Moon'. This entailed sitting upon a large, illuminated crescent moon and being wheeled round the ballroom – on top of which horror, there was someone called Father Christmas lurking in the background, and I was terrified of him. It was with tears on her cheeks that a very unhappy little fairy, wearing a frilly dress, a fluffy white wig and a gold snake bangle, did as she was bidden and endured the harrowing experience.

I was about four years old when something unusual happened. One night I awoke and walked into my parents' room. I went over to the window and opened the curtains. This window, which faced in the opposite direction from mine, overlooked the city, and there was an eerie red glow in the night sky and sparks of golden light shooting upwards. I shook my parents and told them to come and look at the strange lights in the sky; that night, the Theatre Royal was burned to the ground. I had not previously disturbed my parents in the middle of the night, so they were very puzzled as to why I had done so on the night of the fire.

Because of my shyness, my mother hauled me off to the prestigious Constance Grant School of Dancing – she said it would 'broaden me out', whatever that meant. Naturally, I bawled my head off, and Miss Grant remarked, 'Water-bottle will never do a solo or anything else. You are wasting time and money bringing her to classes.' ('Water-bottle' was her pet name for me – for obvious reasons.) However, my mother persevered. She increased my lessons, and before the age of five I had passed all my ballet examinations. I even performed a solo number 'So Shy', at Sheffield's Empire Theatre, much to Miss Grant's amazement, and came off to a roar of applause.

My successes continued and I won trophies and medals in many competitions which included gaining the highest marks, two years running, at the International Dancing Masters Association competition, held annually at Blackpool. (One of the competitors was Glynis Johns who later became a film star.) At the City Hall in Sheffield I won two silver, first-place medals, but then I saw one of the second-place bronze medals. They were a lovely gleaming red-gold colour, so I resolved to win one. In my next dance I deliberately held back a little from giving my all, and thought, 'Bronze, bronze, I want the bronze!', and duly came second. Mother was none too pleased and said, 'You know, you ought to have won the silver, there.' I remained silent, but glowed inside. Was this my first attempt at working magic?

During the Second World War I obtained my first professional engagement, as a Tiller girl in Emile Littler's pantomime *Aladdin* at the Lyceum Theatre in Sheffield. While I was with this company I received a rather unusual initiation into the theatrical profession. The other girls hinted at awful initiation ceremonies – such as covering me from head to toe in greasepaint, cutting off my hair and throwing me into a bath of cold water – and the thought made me nervous every time I entered the stage-door. In the end, Brenda, the head-girl and a decent sort, suggested that I be stripped naked and have blobs of greasepaint daubed all over my body; this sentence was duly carried out and I was then told to leave the room and ask very politely to be allowed in, again. After that they all made much of me; they kissed me, opened a bottle of bubbly, and pronounced me a fully-fledged professional artiste, so it was not too bad, after all. I had no idea then that another initiation, a very different one, awaited me in the future.

It was some time before the German planes arrived over our city, which, like Rome, is built on seven hills. Apparently they were unable to find it, at least according to 'Lord Haw-haw', the radio voice of the German propaganda machine. He was heard on the radio declaring, 'Sheffield is the steel city on wheels. But, never fear, we will find you, Sheffield, and bomb you into the ground!' Whatever the initial difficulties, Hitler's air force duly arrived one evening, with reinforcements, and the Sheffield Blitz had begun. A Luftwaffe pilot, later to die on the Russian front, recorded the raid in his personal diary; describing his first view of the scene, he wrote: 'Below us looks like a sorcerer's cauldron – luminous blobs flashing, brightly glowing smoke . . .' The bombing lasted for many hours, and there were several more raids in the days that followed. The Germans' obvious intention was to find and demolish the Steel Works in the East End of the city. No doubt they knew of the 15-ton steam-hammer at the Vickers works: the only one in the United Kingdom that could forge the crankshafts of the powerful Rolls-Royce Merlin engines for the Hurricanes and Spitfires. Without it, the Battle of Britain, quite literally, would never have got off the ground.

Sheffield's contribution to the war effort was crucial. Strangely enough, only one or two bombs fell on the East End, and the steam-hammer was unharmed. This was mostly due to our Intelligence. The decoy fires and dummy factories in the surrounding countryside, proved most effective!

After the war, my career in the theatre continued apace, and I appeared as principal boy in pantomime, and leading lady in revue, playing most of the theatres in the British Isles. An audition for Barney Colehan at the BBC, resulted in being offered a contract for the then-popular radio programme *Have a Go*, which featured Wilfred Pickles and Violet Carson. I played the city of Birmingham many times, and one week I stayed with a nice couple on the outskirts of the city.

15

Every night the lady's husband met me at the bus-stop and escorted me safely back to their house, taking a short cut across a field. One night there was a very thick fog and my escort was armed with a torch, although it was of very little use in such a pea-souper. We set off across the field, but suddenly I had the feeling that we were walking in the wrong direction, and I also sensed danger. 'Stop!' I shouted, 'Please don't go on. We are going the wrong way.' My companion shone the torch close to the ground, and a short distance ahead, the ground disappeared, with a sheer drop on to a railway line. 'Good God!' he exclaimed, 'I was sure we were on the right path. How on earth did you know?' I said that I didn't know, I just felt the danger. Considerably shaken, we turned away and slowly retraced our steps.

Christmas 1955 saw me happily working as Principal Boy at the Empire, Portsmouth, for the impresario Dick Ray, the uncle of that famous star Peter Sellers. Dick had spoken to me about a new revue he was planning, which was to tour the Moss Empires circuit, and said he would like me to be in it. But, alas, it was not to be. Dick died suddenly, and my life was about to change, dramatically.

The next year, 1956, was to prove important and fateful for me in many ways and coincided with Saturn's return in my birth-chart. (Briefly, it takes this planet 29 years to travel round the Zodiac and return to the position it occupied at the time of birth. This transit usually brings important transformations in a person's life, and it did for me.) I returned home to Sheffield, and a friend called round and took me out to the cinema. During the interval we were treated to the usual advertisements, one of which was for Sharps toffees: it showed a man in a white coat standing behind a counter and serving the said toffees to the accompaniment of the jingle: 'Sharps, the word for toffee; Sharps, the word for toffee'. Three months later, when I met the man who eventually became my husband, I learned that he was the person in the advertisement!

My dear father died in the spring. It was a sorrowful time for my mother and me, and relatives invited us down to Great Bookham in Surrey for a rest, but soon I received a call from an agent offering me a summer season on the Isle of Wight. I was the only breadwinner at the time, so I accepted, albeit reluctantly, and my Uncle and Aunt suggested that I stay with them during rehearsals in London. When, in due course I did so, Uncle Norman commented that there was someone in 'my' show whom he knew quite well: Arnold Crowther, a stage magician and (like himself) a Freemason, who often entertained at Masonic functions. I explained that we were rehearsing the musical numbers at Dineley's Studios, so I had yet to meet all the company.

However, one day a tall man entered the room and came straight across to me. 'Are you a Libran?' he asked. Slightly surprised I said I was. Then another question, 'Are you interested in the Occult?' I laughed. 'I suppose I am.' With that he smiled at me, turned on his heel, and departed as suddenly as he had appeared. 'How odd,' I thought. 'What unusual questions to ask a stranger. And how did he know I was a Libran?' The incident was soon forgotten in the flurry of rehearsals, and it was not until much later – when I met Arnold Crowther 'officially' – that I recalled something which had happened the previous year, when I was working in Birmingham. I had been staying with a lovely lady called Nita, who read the cards professionally, and I asked her if she would read them for me. She told me that I would meet my future husband over water, and that his name would be Arnold. Nita was also clairvoyant and told me many things that subsequently came true, and in the course of time I took Arnold to meet her.

At the Pier Casino theatre in Shanklin, Arnold took charge of the morning matinées for the children, and he asked me if I would play the piano at these shows. This gave us the opportunity for closer acquaintance, and conversations over coffee or lunch at a local restaurant. I wanted to know why he had asked me such curious questions in the rehearsal rooms. He said it was because he had recognized me as someone he had known in a previous life. He was positive we had met in Ancient Egypt! I said that surely we had looked different all those centuries ago and might have been of the opposite sex. He agreed, but pointed out that there is an indefinable 'something' that remembers, attracts, and draws souls together again.

One day I showed Arnold a book I was reading; it had

caught my eye in the window of a bookshop, and on an impulse I had popped in and bought it. The title was *Witchcraft Today*, and the author was a man called Gerald Gardner. 'But I know Gerald Gardner,' exclaimed Arnold. 'He's an old friend of mine.' He went on to tell me how he had met Gerald in 1939 in London, at a lecture on folklore given by Christina Hole, and had subsequently been invited to his flat where he met Gerald's charming wife Donna. She enquired if he would take tiffin with them (Donna often spoke in the idiom of the Far East, having lived with her husband in Malaya for many years).

I listened with great interest as Arnold told me how Gerald once took him to the home of a lady called Vanda. She frequently held soirées where various artistes, intellectuals and writers, were able to commune with their equals and let down their hair by 'peeling off', as Gerald put it, and sitting around sky-clad. I gazed at him open-mouthed, 'And you actually took off your clothes in the company of strangers?' Arnold laughed, 'Yes, but it was all quite innocent I assure you.' I was all ears to know more. And what was 'sky-clad'? I learned that this was a term Gerald used when in the company of non-witches; it actually meant being naked.

Arnold was often invited to the Gardners' flat, and Gerald once gave him some old swords in which Arnold had expressed an interest. As he carried his new possessions, inadequately wrapped, on the London Underground, an old man accosted him, ''Ello mate. Just been demobbed from the Boer War?'

I also learned that just before World War II, Arnold's agent rang to say he had a booking for him at a very special children's party. When Arnold asked for the address, the agent laughed, 'Well, you can't miss it. It's the most famous building in London. How does Buckingham Palace appeal to you?' The party was held for the then Princesses Elizabeth and Margaret Rose. After that Arnold found his services in demand from members of the aristocracy, and he became known as a 'society entertainer'.

Arnold and I very soon became 'an item', and he wrote to Gerald telling his friend all the news. Gardner replied, inviting us to visit him at Castletown in the Isle of Man, where he ran his famous museum of witchcraft. However, due to professional engagements, it was some time before we were able to accept the invitation.

Islands are said to be lucky for Librans, and I found this to be true. I had adored the season I spent on Anglesey and enjoyed great success, there. And the Isle of Wight had brought me romance with a capital 'R', so I was agog to know what the Isle of Man had in store. I was not disappointed, because it proved to hold the most extraordinary experiences of them all!

2   Curiouser and Curiouser . . .

The blindfold was whisked away and I blinked in the gentle glow of candlelight. My initiation into the Mysteries of the Goddess had just taken place. With sword held high, my Initiator stood before me, his tall, sun-tanned body and snow-white hair, reflecting the lambent flames. He looked the very epitome of the consecrated High Priest.

That night, as the wind buffeted against the windows of the barn, and the only other sounds were the slow, plop-plop of the paraffin stoves, his considerable age lay lightly upon him. Gerald Gardner looked at me, a smile upon his lips and questions in his eyes. I guessed that he was wondering how the ceremony had affected me and if I would be strong enough to overcome the tests that initiation always brings.

Initiation into any school of magic invokes certain trials, involving both body and soul. This tempering is not achieved through easy living, but through adversity and certain suffering (although, it is said that initiates are never given more than can be endured in one incarnation); much depends upon the aspects of the Natal chart. In the Priesthood of the Old Religion, the Goddess will watch over you as a mother watches over her children. If you succeed, She will gradually improve your circumstances, and things will begin to move in the required direction. After thirty-seven years in the Craft, I can fully endorse this philosophy.

I smiled back at the High Priest and suddenly knew him very well, indeed. A spark of recognition ignited between us; I had known this soul in the distant past. It was the awakening of old memories, evoked by the ritual. Initiation can also arouse psychic abilities and always brings a new appreciation of Self.

Providing that the Initiate has reached a certain maturity, the seeking for hidden knowledge will breed wisdom and a broadening on all levels of consciousness, which is entirely necessary for soul development. When initiation is achieved, the call goes out on the Inner Planes that someone has set their feet upon The Path.

After a short rest I was required to initiate Arnold into the Mysteries. (Gerald said that years before, when Arnold had expressed an interest in the Craft, he had told him, 'You *will* be initiated, but not yet. You must wait for a fair-haired young woman to do that for you – and she'll be damned pretty, too!' So the prophecy came to pass – although I would hesitate to confirm how I appear to others.) When all had been accomplished, the three of us sat in the now cosy atmosphere of the Circle, passing round the Communal Horn Cup. Gerald talked to us about magic, and that night I learned many things.

It was still very difficult for me to believe what had happened since I met Gerald Gardner at his home in Malew Street, Castletown (the story of which I have told elsewhere). For me, it was like stepping into a different world: a magical world, that had existed for hundreds of years behind the mundanity of everyday life. From what Gerald said, these people, the witches, were interesting, intelligent folk, who only wanted what was best for themselves and others. This was in complete contrast to the picture of them put over by the Christian Church.

Gerald told me that, when working magic, the *timing* of a rite was very important, and that the Four Tides of the year should be taken into consideration. An ideal time lay between the summer solstice and the autumn equinox, when nature has reached her greatest potential and the etheric emanations are strongest. A time when they could most profitably be tapped. This, he said, was why the witches in the New Forest had chosen Lammas to work against Hitler's proposed invasion of Britain. It was also the reason why the ritual was performed *in the forest*, on Lammas Eve, 1940, *when the Moon was in the last days of her waning*. The ideal time for getting rid of something! The date, time of year, the phase of the Moon and the site were as conducive as they were ever likely to be for such a fateful ritual. A ritual that became known as 'Operation Cone of Power'!

Historians of World War II have stated that only two things stopped *Operation Sealion* (Hitler's plan for the invasion of Britain) from being carried out. One was the Battle of Britain, which took place in the air, and the other was the Führer's unexpected and inexplicable change of plan, to move East and invade Russia. At one of my lectures, a young man mentioned that he had read in a book about the war that Hitler dozed off during a meeting of some sort – something previously unheard of. When he woke up, he suddenly announced that he was aborting *Operation Sealion* for the time being and informed his astonished officers of his decision to invade Russia, instead. The German war machine was immediately deployed towards this other objective, and Britain heaved a sigh of relief. But I wonder if this was the way the magic was manifested. Could Hitler's forty winks have been the Magical Sleep through which the *intent* of the witches became implanted in his mind?

In *Witchcraft Today*, Gerald says:

> I saw a very interesting ceremony performed with the intention of putting a certain idea into his [Hitler's] mind, and *this was repeated several times afterwards* [my emphasis]; and though all the invasion barges were ready, the fact was that Hitler never even tried to come.

He also tells us:

> Mighty Forces were used, of which I may not speak. Now to do this means using one's life-force; and many of us died a few days after we did this. My asthma, which I have never had since I first went out East, came back badly. We repeated the ritual four times; and the Elders said: 'We feel we have stopped him. We must not kill too many of our people. Keep them until we need them.'

The repetitions of the ritual were to make it even stronger and more sure, and, as Gerald told me, took place soon after the initial rite in order to keep up the momentum of the magic. In matters of grave importance such as this, the success of the rituals was imperative *for the good of all.*

Similar magic was performed by our ancestors to stop Napoleon's invasion of Britain and to impede the Spanish Armada. In the case of the Armada, the ships were halfway across the Channel before the danger was discovered – apparently, surprise tactics had been employed – so covens had to rely upon raising winds to cause storms at sea. And great storms *did* occur, which scattered the Armada; many of the ships were blown off course and were lost on the coasts of Scotland and Ireland (their wrecks are still being discovered today). Others scuttled back to the safety of the Spanish ports.

At various times in Britain's history, witches and magicians have used their skills against a common enemy. It would be wrong to assume otherwise. Sir Francis Drake was considered by some to have been a member of the witch cult in Devon. A well-known headland in Plymouth is called Devil's Point, which the locals say was a witches' meeting-place, hence the name. Whatever the truth about Drake and witchcraft, the ghostly phenomenon known as 'Drakes Drum' was heard during World Wars I and II.

During one of our many trips to the Isle of Man, some 'young' witches came to Gerald's house wanting to know more about magic. They sat at the feet of the famous Elder, drinking in his words, and with Gerald's permission, I took down the conversation in shorthand, and this is what he said:

People always ask me, 'Why do you want to be a witch? Why should anyone want to become a witch? What do you get out of it?' When I tell them you get peace and contentment and joy, they can't understand that. They want to know, 'Don't you make money out of it?' Well, I say, you don't. 'Well, you must. You must make money – you make spells to get yourself money.' I say, 'You don't, we are taught the power comes from the Gods. It must not be misused.' You can misuse your power all right, but you'll lose it if you do. So it's just as plain as that.

Of course, it isn't a thing that belongs to everybody. Some

people have a sense of the old things, a desire for peace, a sense of wonder, and a sense of companionship and good fellowship, and that's what witchcraft gives you.

A pretty, auburn-haired girl wanted to know the secret of obtaining magical power and how to work magic. Gerald replied:

Yes, well . . . simply, when I want to do it . . . (Patricia here does it – she knows it) . . . you've got to know *exactly* what you want. You've got to get it into your mind exactly what you want. It's not a vague thing: 'I want John Jones to get well.' You must know what's the matter with him. What particular part of him you want to treat. You've got to fix *that* very firmly in your mind. And you've got to get the people who are helping to know what you are working at.

Then, of course, it's a question of raising your nerve power. Well, there are many ways of raising nerve power. Of course the simplest and possibly the oldest one is dancing round – and, actually, yelling and screaming helps. But, of course, it's a thing that is apt to take your mind off things, and I simply . . . I have not the breath to dance, so I've got to work in other ways. But there are a number of ways you can work magic. I don't want to go into that because you will be taught, and these are secrets.

Of course, another way – a very old way of working magic – is the Hindu Yoga thing – that is, a method of intense concentration: fixing your mind on the thing; sitting there. You've got to get yourself into one of these Yoga positions – immobilize yourself. Forget your body, only concentrate on that one thought and work on that – work on that; will and will and will and will – and, of course, they say it works. I don't know whether it does. I never tried it; it's too much like hard work to me.

But, of course, the thing is to try the form of magic that appeals to you, and find out if it works. I think the Yoga system is too apt to lead to illusions. I don't doubt that people get great pleasure out of it, because the concentration produces the effect of an opium dream. They have wonderful illusions, and they enjoy themselves very greatly. If that's all you want from it, it's

24

a cheap way of doing it. Of course, a lot of my countrymen do the same thing with a couple of bottles of whiskey! Of course, sometimes they have a headache the morning after.

On one of our trips to see Gerald, the ballroom at the Witches' Mill was due to be opened. It was constructed on the ground floor, between the restaurant and the ruined mill, and Gerald asked us if we would provide the cabaret on the opening night. Having had no prior notice of the event, I believe I borrowed an accordion from somewhere, while Arnold purloined a large mandrake root from the museum for his ventriloquial act. A mouth was made by applying lipstick to his forefinger and thumb, with a little wig and painted eyes, slipped on to his other fingers. Then, by holding a 'body' dressed in a suit, he created 'Andy'. Not having his props with him, the mandrake root became the body, and by moving the 'mouth' (Arnold's finger and thumb), 'Andy' could speak, smoke, and even put out his tongue!

In *Lid off the Cauldron* I mentioned that Gerald was convinced that something of importance always happened to him every nine years (in occultism, the number of the Moon), and I also pointed out that the museum was sold nine years after his death. It would appear that this cycle is still in operation, for nine years after the museum was sold, Geoffrey Basil Smith, then Grand Master of the now defunct anti-Crowley M.A.A.T. (Master of the Argenteum Temple) Lodge of the Ordo Templi Orientis,* resurrected Gerald's charter. A photograph of it appears in his work, *Knights of the Solar Cross* (printed by Evans of the Kinder Press, New Mills, Nr. Stockport, Cheshire, 1983), in which the author is described as 'Grand Master of the M.A.A.T. Egyptian lodge, 1983'. The charter reads:

Do What Thou Wilt Shall Be the Law. We Baphomet X°, Degree Ordo Templi Orientis Sovereign Grand Master

* Inaugurated under the authority provided by Dr Gardner's OTO 'Camp' charter, and the conclusions underlining this, which were reached by Frater Transmutemini in Francis King's *The Secret Rituals of the O.T.O.* (C.W. Daniel Co, London, 1973).

General of all English Speaking countries of the Earth, do hereby Authorise our beloved son, Scire, (Dr G.B. Gardner), Prince of Jerusalem, to constitute a camp of the 'Ordo Templi Orientis', in the degree Minerval. Love is the law, love under will.

Witness my hand and seal
Baphomet X°

This document is affixed with four wax seals and ribbons which bear designs and inscriptions. In some places it is written in blood, and on the reverse side is a land document and will from the County of Surrey which is dated 1875. This was the year of Crowley's birth, and was also the year which saw the foundation of the Theosophical Society.

The above charter was displayed in Gerald's museum and was given to him by Aleister Crowley. My late husband, Arnold Crowther, took Gardner to meet Crowley in 1946 and Crowley gave Arnold a signed copy of his book of poetry, entitled *Olla*, which is now in my possession. *Olla* was printed by the O.T.O. and limited to 500 copies.

In *Knights of the Solar Cross*, Smith describes a dream he had.

Several years ago, I had a dream about San Francisco (named after Saint Francis), which, for no clear reason, I then associated with Fishermen's Wharf. The meaning became clearer when I later discovered that, after Crowley's death, there were several individuals in England who were members of the OTO, but only one person who was chartered to conduct a 'camp' of the order: Gerald Gardner, the leader of many British witches.

Geoff Smith paid me a visit, and during our conversation, he mentioned how many occultists regarded me as Gerald Gardner's spiritual heir – surprising, yet heart-warming news. It was because of this, and Gerald's link with the OTO, that Geoff Smith, as the then Grand Master of that Order, was able to bestow upon me the title, 'Honorary High Priestess of M.A.A.T.'. This was a curious twist of fate, as I had been performing the rites of this Egyptian goddess for some time.

Smith asked me if I could throw any light upon a place called 'Fishermen's Wharf' in San Francisco, and I told him that, when Gerald's museum was sold to Ripley's Believe It or Not! organization in the US, it was transferred to Fishermen's Wharf in San Francisco! Geoff Smith received this information with glee, as it confirmed the veracity of his dream.

The Museum of Witchcraft and Magic is now defunct, as the contents were later distributed to become part of various other Ripley-owned ventures, and some of the collection was even sold to private buyers. I often wonder what became of the little 'demon' that used to sit in a triangle in Gerald's museum. Arnold created it from papier mâché then buried it for a time to make it look suitably gruesome. (Gerald used to say that it had become very big-headed, due to having its picture taken so often.)

One case in the museum was of great interest to me. Among other items it contained a large wooden box with a mirror inside the lid and paintings of the God and Goddess on either side. It held a miscellany of vials, charms, talismans and knives, and the latter had curious signs incised upon them. Referring to this item, the text of the museum's explanatory pamphlet read: 'A large number of objects belonging to a witch who died in 1951, lent by her relatives, who wish to remain anonymous. These are mostly things which had been used in the family for generations . . .'. These artefacts had belonged to Gerald's initiator, Dorothy Fordham, who died on the 12 January, 1951.

Since his own death in 1964 Gerald Gardner has been accused times without number of inventing 'Old Dorothy', as she was known to her intimates. This is just another way of implying that he never achieved initiation into the Craft. However, through the efforts of Doreen Valiente, the identity of Dorothy St Quintin Fordham (née Clutterbuck), has been verified! With the recovery of her birth and death certificates, and of course her will, Gerald's claim has been validated. Amazingly, even more evidence about 'Old Dorothy' has come to light. A newspaper article from the *Bournemouth Evening Echo* dated 25 February 1986, and headed 'Illustrated 1942 Diaries "Find" on show', contains this revealing information:

Bournemouth art school student Helen Bassett has unearthed a treasure trove of local social history in a cupboard of clutter. While rummaging among obsolete files and old papers at the solicitor's office where she worked as a secretary, Helen discovered a charming three-part diary, lovingly illustrated in watercolours. Her employers would have thrown out the wartime diary with the rubbish, but artistic Helen realised its worth, and retrieved it from the bin. Now she hopes the handwritten books of verses and pictures will be published, like Edith Holden's best-selling Country Diary.

The diaries give a vivid insight into the leisured life of the wealthy Mrs Dorothy Fordham who owned two magnificent houses near Chewton Glen at Highcliffe; the Mill House and Lattimers. Mrs Fordham, a copious writer of verse on subjects as diverse as gas masks and stately architecture, collaborated with her friend, Mrs Christine Wells, who illustrated the poetry. Mrs Fordham displays a mischievous sense of humour in the verse, rarely dwelling on the grim reality of the war. (Wearing a gas mask becomes a good method of avoiding onerous conversation – in one poem!)

Helen, a graphic design student at DIHE, Wallisdown, and her friend, Mr Kenneth Harvey-Packer, have mounted an exhibition of the 1942-3 diaries at Lansdowne Library. The Exhibition will be on show in London during April.

In Dorothy's last Will and Testament, she conveyed her wish to be cremated and for her ashes to be buried in the grave of Rupert Oswald Fordham, in the churchyard at Highcliffe. Recently, while on holiday in the New Forest, I searched the churchyard at Highcliffe to find Rupert Fordham's grave. The first time I had no luck, but after retiring for the night, I suddenly heard Gerald's voice in my head, saying, 'You must look under the trees. It's beside the trees.'

The next morning I returned to the graveyard. The tombstones were old and the grass overgrown between them so that it was difficult to read the inscriptions. Thinking of Gerald's words, I walked over to some graves overhung by trees and, sure enough, there it was, just as my friend had said: a tall, granite column, surmounted with a Celtic cross and decorated with triform Celtic knots. The large, square base carried the inscription: 'In ever dearest and most beloved memory of Rupert Oswald, deeply loved husband of Dorothy St Quintin Fordham who passed away May 31st 1939 aged 77 years.' Beneath these words there followed a verse. I could find no inscription for Dorothy, herself, but here is where her ashes are buried.

When Rupert Fordham died aged 77, we know that Dorothy was 59 years old, a difference of *eighteen* years (that Moon number, again: $1+8=9$). Curiously, the same difference in age as between Arnold and me! In that quiet place I thought of Gerald and his friends Dorothy and Rupert. Then, deeper into the past, to those witches who had brought Dorothy (and Rupert?) to the Goddess – the ancestors! I marvelled at the lineage that I and other witches had inherited and were honour bound to pass on. I bought some everlasting flowers, wondering how long it had been since the grave was last tended. Many years, no doubt. I hope that other witches will find it and replace my flowers with fresh ones.

This link with the past reminded me of a time in the seventies, when I was with witch friends in the Isle of Man. They took me to the churchyard where Donna Gardner's remains are buried. It may have been pure chance, but I walked straight through the graves, and stopped in front of Donna's. A pentagram in a circle crowns the headstone, and beneath the inscription to Donna is one dedicated to Gerald Gardner. (Gerald died abroad, but his friends on the Isle of Man considered it only right and proper to place a memorial to him, on Donna's grave. His mortal remains rest in a cemetery close to Carthage, on the North African coast. Carthage! One of the most celebrated cities of the ancient world, and the religious centre for the worship of the Great Mother Goddess! Perhaps, the most fitting place for such a devoted follower of the Goddess to find peace.)

In 1988 I was again on the Isle of Man, and I searched all the shops to find some colourful, plastic flowers for the grave. I wanted something that would last and look cheerful, and plastic flowers would fit the bill. I struck lucky in one shop, where the assistant said she thought they had some put away, upstairs. She returned with an armful of bright red blooms, and stems of copper-coloured leaves. They were perfect! I also purchased some silk flowers, but knew that however pretty they looked, their colours would soon fade. The grave had a cared-for look about it, when I took my leave.

On 9 November 1960, five months after we were initiated into the Craft, Arnold and I were married. Gerald flew over (by plane!) for the wedding, and the night before the civil ceremony, he performed the rite of 'Handfasting' for us. (This ancient rite binds two people together, but only for as long as their love for one another endures. If, unhappily, their love wanes, they have a duty to be honest with one another, talk the matter over in the Circle, then, if possible, agree to part as friends.) Gerald thought that in many ways it was a good idea to be legally joined in wedlock – not least because we were living in my mother's home at the time! We were away for long periods, so it was just not feasible to buy or rent a property that would stand empty for months on end, and, although Mother was a broad-minded lady for her generation, she drew the line at her daughter 'living in sin', as she put it, under her own roof.

In the years that followed, my mother read more about the Old Religion and discussed it with us. In this way, she came to recognize and love the Goddess, and, being the perfect hostess, she would welcome the 'seekers' who came along and make them feel at home. A true Leo lady. Mother also helped to create a temple in the house and decorated it herself with a stone-effect wallpaper which blended well with the oak beams and gave the necessary atmosphere.

There could have been two weddings in our family, and fairly close together, because Gerald Gardner proposed marriage to my mother. He hastily reassured her it would be a union of companionship and friendship only, but, although my mother regarded Gerald as a close friend and someone upon whom she could rely, she did not want to leave her home and the environment in which she lived. They would go off together for tea in town, and got on like a house on fire. I know that she was very concerned about hurting her friend's feelings, but she felt unable to make such a major change at that late stage in her life.

Initially, it must have been difficult for my mother to accept the idea of witchcraft, and when I announced that I was an initiated witch she must have wondered what on earth it was all about. She was often stopped in the street by people she had known for years, enquiring, 'What's it about, Mrs Dawson? Do they worship the Devil?' and so on. I think she was often upset by such remarks, but she always stood up for me and put them straight, telling them that I worshipped the Great Goddess.

The day before our wedding, the fourth estate put in an appearance. There must have been at least twenty cars lined up outside our house, and the resulting reports, in both local and national newspapers, were perfectly acceptable. The story soon achieved world-wide coverage as it filtered through the various news agencies. Being in the theatrical profession, we were not embarrassed by so much publicity; it was nothing new to us. However, this was the first time there had ever been a 'Witches' Wedding', as the press called it.

For the big day I wore a black velvet suit, a spray of orchids, and a delicate purple satin cap with a small veil. From my handbag hung a talisman of Venus (constructed by Gerald), and I carried the carved wand he had presented to me at my initiation, which he insisted I should hold. He made vague allusions to the phallic potency of the symbol, which I thought was fair enough. And I must point out that in due course, the wand was reconsecrated and returned to the altar.

I did not consider the significance of wearing black to my wedding – it just happened to be a suit that I liked – but it fired the journalists' imagination. 'The Bride will be dressed in Black when two witches Wed', 'In Thunder, Lightning or in Rain – the Witches will Wed', and 'Chief's Spell seals Married Witches' Happiness' were some of the headlines that day. The press regarded Gerald as the chief witch of Britain, and one picture showed him blessing us by holding the wand over our heads.

We had ordered a limousine from the local funeral directors to take us to the registry office. Again we had not seen anything untoward in our choice of vehicle; the director was a friend of my mother's, and the firm often hired out cars for occasions other than funerals. However, when we were being driven into the city, I noticed a sign in one of the windows, which read 'C & A Reed, Funeral Directors', and we giggled all the way to our destination.

In the city centre, newspaper vendors' placards proclaimed, 'The Witches are to Wed', and Gerald was highly amused at all the attention we were receiving and enjoyed himself, hugely. After the ceremony, the press followed us to the Grand Hotel, where a celebratory luncheon had been planned but, before we were allowed to eat, flash bulbs continued to pop merrily as yet more pictures were taken. Mother was quite put out because she wanted a photograph of the family but found that the press were only interested in the witches. She retired in high dudgeon until I asked a local photographer to oblige, then all was well.

For months afterwards, reporters beat a path to our door. It seemed that witchcraft was suddenly worthy of recognition. I never imagined that a public notice of my forthcoming marriage would develop into such a newsworthy feature, and on such a far-reaching scale. The television people became interested, and we appeared on a variety of programmes, making our debut on *People & Places* from Granada TV in Manchester. This was followed by *Look North, Calendar, Nationwide,* and *Twenty-four Hours,* along with radio programmes and documentaries including *A Welkin of Witchcraft* and *The Evil Eye,* the latter featuring such celebrities as Robert Graves and Christina Hole.

Michael Barton, then controller of BBC Radio Sheffield, invited us to present a series of six weekly programmes on the subject. Our producer was Peter Hawkins, and he proved to be extremely sympathetic and helped to make the endeavour both varied and interesting. A great deal of work went into this venture – the first series on witchcraft to be broadcast in Britain. Each twenty-minute episode dealt with a different aspect of the Old Religion and was recorded in the dead of night when the station was more or less 'sleeping'. Other witches took part and discussed their views and/or psychic experiences, and people whom we had helped through magic talked about how our work had affected their lives in the solving of particular problems. Hill-figures, stone circles, the

Witch Persecutions, and the renaissance of the Craft of the Wise, were some of the aspects also addressed, with background music and sound effects imparting the correct atmosphere.

When Peter required lines to be spoken in a particular accent, as if by magic, a person with the right qualifications would arrive at the studio to fulfil his needs, even though the reason for their presence at Radio Sheffield, had nothing to do with our programme. Thus, an actor from Suffolk took the part of Matthew Hopkins, the Witchfinder General, and a Scottish presenter spoke the lines of King James I, and read an extract from Robert Burns' famous poem, 'Tam o' Shanter', which describes a meeting of witches at the Old Kirk in Alloway.

A Spell of Witchcraft (Arnold's title) went out on 6 January 1971, and Michael Barton declared it to be a resounding success. BBC Television, Scotland, based in Glasgow, then decided to record a pilot programme on witchcraft and asked us to take part in it, along with a coven from Edinburgh, and various occultists and clairvoyants from that region. We were interviewed by Magnus Magnusson, the presenter of *Mastermind*, in front of an invited studio audience which included the scientist and TV personality, Magnus Pike. All went well, until Magnus introduced the aspect of nudity into the proceedings, by asking me if nudity had an effect upon the members of a coven, in respect of sexual arousal (much sniggering from audience). My reply was somewhat lengthy, as I pointed out that a partially clothed person was far more likely to arouse carnal desires than a naked one (most people tend to look more attractive when wearing clothes). I also added that the rituals tended to *raise* the consciousness and procure a state of mind beyond the physical, although it would appear from the question, that there was some room for improvement in his (Magnus's) case. The audience went wild, and the programme never saw the light of day; not least because a witch had verbally trounced a highly regarded presenter!

I liked Magnus as a person, and after the show he told me with pride that he was a true pagan, being descended from a long line of Icelanders. He paid me one of the nicest compli-

33

ments I have ever had, when he confided, 'I have met many women, but it's the first time I have met a female.'

Back at the hotel, we had a lovely get-together with the Edinburgh witches, and due to a sudden loss of electricity, we sat in candlelight, drinking wine and enjoying a very 'Merry Meet'!

Speaking of compliments, while playing in Newcastle-upon-Tyne, I was asked to take part in a radio programme entitled *Voice of the People*, and Harold Williamson came to my dressing-room to make the recording. He observed that I had the bluest eyes he had ever seen, which was strange because, as I remarked, I was just about to say the same thing about his! What one might call a mutual admiration society!

A request for our services as witches came from Tyne-Tees Television's news programme, *North East Roundabout*. The television crew came to the theatre and filmed the piece on the stage, but, as in most interviews of this nature, our theatrical work was never discussed. I mention this because in the early days of our commitment to the Craft a certain individual commented to Gerald that the Crowthers appeared in the media, talking about witchcraft, simply in order to boost their professional engagements. This was complete nonsense. We always obtained our work on the strength of our professional reputation, and both Arnold and I were established performers long before we came to the Craft. Gerald's informant merely revealed a total ignorance of the theatrical profession and how it works.

On yet another visit to the Tyne-Tees studios we had a run-through before 'going live', and I was asked, 'Is it not a little unusual, this witchcraft?' I said that it was no more unusual than say, *Coronation Street*, whereupon the technicians fell about – mainly, I think, because 'the Street' was the product of a rival TV company. Still, the comment had the effect intended, as the question was omitted from the transmission.

Some time later a letter appeared in the *Sheffield Star*, headed 'Television witch-hunt', and stated that a Mr Jack Clarke from Tyne-Tees Television, was producing a new series, *The David Jacobs Show* and wished to contact a witch who lived in Sheffield to appear on it. The witch, he said, had appeared for him in a programme some years before and 'is very striking, tall and fair-haired'. Well, I thought modestly, it must be me, and I contacted Mr Clarke forthwith. As a result, both Arnold and I were booked for one of the programmes, along with the Labour MP Tom Driberg, whose claim to fame in the magical field was confined to owning a diary which had belonged to Aleister Crowley.

During the interview, Driberg produced a large card with white lines upon it. This, he said, was the curse Crowley had designed for Norman Mudd, one of his disciples. Showing the card to the studio audience and the cameras, he commented that the drawing meant Mudd would drown in deep water. My mind skimmed frivolously – surely water *created* mud – and then the song, 'Mud, mud, glorious mud!' . . . I managed to glimpse the card and exclaimed, 'But, that is a hexagram of the *I Ching*, and I believe it is the hexagram of Earth and Water. It sounds more like a prophesy than a curse.' Driberg, ever so slightly ruffled, replied, 'It must have been a curse, because that was the way in which Norman Mudd died.' Arnold interjected, saying that it was the first time he had heard of the *I Ching* being associated with a curse and, having met Crowley, he did not think it was at all in the style of the 'Great Beast'.

David Jacobs, who had commented earlier that he knew nothing about witchcraft or the occult, contributed nothing to the discussion; he merely smiled blandly and seemed uneasy during the entire proceedings. Driberg ignored us afterwards. We had apparently stood on one of his favourite corns, although I cannot say that this worried us unduly.

I received invitations to talk to a wide variety of societies and clubs, as well as the universities of Sheffield, Leeds, Manchester and Liverpool (to date, they number around three hundred). The size of audiences differed immensely; one of the largest consisted of roughly a thousand students, while the smallest, in a private house, consisted of three ladies and a dog – the dog seemed to enjoy it, too.

The lectures at Sheffield University were for various departments, but the most daunting took place in the Lower Refectory Hall before a vast, seething mass of students. Nevertheless, it resulted in a further invitation for the following year; on both occasions the hall was packed, and the gallery walk that runs above it was crammed with a sea of faces. It is the custom in some universities to give the speaker dinner before the talk – rather like a condemned prisoner eating his last meal. (Of course, I would have preferred something to eat *after* the address, when the nerves had settled down, but this only occurred at the University of Liverpool.) With all eyes upon me, I walked through the hall and on to the dais, preceded by a professor in his flowing robes and mortar-board, who then introduced me. Other professors occupied the front row. I must say that the students were very attentive; it is always a bonus, in a large hall, when everyone can hear you. At the end, much to my relief, the applause was deafening.

It was time for questions from the floor, and one student stood up and declared that he did not believe in witches. This caused another student to call out, 'Be quiet! You know f... all about it!' Arnold later commented, 'Well, okay, he swore, but *he* was on your side!' That was perfectly true.

Without being pompous, I realize that I have a good image for the public face of witchcraft: a student commented to a reporter in Leeds that I looked more like a good fairy than a witch. I always said that, if they expected me to have warts, a nutcracker face and straggly hair, then they must invite me back in another thirty years, when I might be able to oblige them!

I am aware that I am invited to speak to people because of their avid curiosity about witchcraft. Some folk, after listening to the bleatings of their local vicar, are very disappointed to hear little of black magic or the defiling of virgins (I do stress, though, that the latter are very few and far between these days.) I knock popular misconceptions about witches and what they get up to very firmly on the head, and also take care to inform an audience that the Craft is the priesthood of the Old Religion, which acknowledges the Great Goddess and Her Consort. In the Middle Ages the insidious propaganda machine of the Christian Church firmly entrenched in the minds of its followers the idea that witches worshipped the Devil, and many people are still loath to abandon that opinion.

A telephone call from a lady with a very refined voice

informed me that she was the speaker-finder for the National Women's Association of Great Britain. Would I be willing to address them after luncheon, at their annual meeting in London? I agreed. The venue was a large, beautiful, oak-beamed hall that had once belonged to Sir Thomas More; transported from its original site, it now overlooks the river Thames in the heart of London. It was all very grand, and the ladies, two hundred of them, were dressed in the height of fashion and wore large-brimmed, colourful hats. I had anticipated the tone of the affair, and completed my outfit with a large fake-fur beret. The company, as one might expect, were extremely conservative in their outlook and most of them wore frosty expressions during my lecture. However, the social graces were present throughout, and any claws were very carefully sheathed.

When I was guest speaker for the Tewkesbury and Evesham Townswomen's Guild, the meeting yielded surprising consequences. It was the occasion of the town's centenary celebrations of the Battle of Tewkesbury. We had spent the previous day in Cheltenham with our friends Bill and Bobbie Gray, and as I drove the four of us to Tewkesbury we had a very close call which could have proved fatal. We were motoring along a straight stretch of road, when a car appeared travelling in the opposite direction – fine! Then another vehicle came into view and started to overtake the first. The driver was not going to make it back into his own lane; he had miscalculated the distance and was heading straight for us. I swerved, violently, on to the grass verge, braked and managed to gain the road again. We had missed a collision by a hair's breadth. The incident is interesting, in view of what was to follow.

At the Watson Hall in Tewkesbury Mrs M. Ackworth, the chairperson of the Guild, informed us that church leaders had been up in arms about my forthcoming talk; there had been articles in the papers saying how they disapproved of a witch giving a lecture on witchcraft, (though it might have been acceptable if the speaker had been someone other than a witch). The public was also invited to the talk, as well as members of the Townswomen's Guild, and two hundred tickets had been sold. Church leaders thought there would be some sort of demonstration, and that the talk would be cancelled, but everything proceeded as planned, with the Lord Mayor and the Lady Mayoress sitting in the front row.

When I had finished speaking, a man in the audience stood up – according to the papers, he was Derek Gitsham, a member of a religious fellowship from Exeter. Because I had announced that the Craft does not seek converts, he wanted to know why I had come to Tewkesbury to talk about it. I pointed out that my lecture had been given at the request of the Townswomen's Guild, and that surely religious beliefs could be expressed without expecting people to adopt them – that was nonsense.

Afterwards we were invited to dine with some ladies from the Guild. They protested strongly about the attitude of the Church, and Mrs Ackworth's views – that this was a free country, and that people could speak on what subjects they liked – had already appeared in the press. It was the most controversial happening Tewkesbury had seen for many years, and there was more to come!

The following day the story made front-page headlines in the *Gloucestershire Echo*, and subsequent issues carried letters for and against witchcraft. A cartoon appeared of a vicar and his wife staring at a frog sitting at a dinner table. The 'frog's' wife, with crossed arms and a frown on her face, was saying, 'The last thing he remembers is being rude to some strange woman as he drove through Tewkesbury.'

Two separate reports, one of which appeared before the talk, gave us much food for thought. The *Gloucestershire Echo* carried an article headed 'Tewkesbury Church Leaders hit at Witch', describing how people were meeting to discuss ways of trying to stop me giving the talk. One church leader, pastor Colin Sinclair of Prior's Park Chapel, said that the ministers were fasting and praying throughout the day. Another article in the *Western Daily Press* announced that 'Tewkesbury ministers fasted and prayed throughout yesterday to ward off the evil powers which they thought were associated with Mrs Crowther's visit.'

Now, prayer and intent, combined with fasting to aid the concentration, is a magical procedure of the most negative kind. It has been known throughout history and is usually

38

performed to cause misfortune or even death to the victim; hence it used to be feared and called, 'The Black Fast'. It can hardly be assumed that the ministers were ignorant of the nature of such a ritual. They obviously knew its significance and, what is more, used it deliberately. I wondered at the time why a Guild lady said to me, 'Your gods must be stronger than the Christian God, as you performed the lecture, after all.' Now I knew! I also remembered the narrow escape we had in the car that day. Was it the outcome of a black magic rite performed by Christian priests? If so, there would appear to be more than a modicum of truth in the Guild Lady's comment.

Letters started to pour in requesting aid on many diverse matters, but we nearly always chose those concerning ill-health upon which to concentrate. There is only so much magic that two witches can accomplish over a short period of time, as it requires using one's life force. So it is very necessary for the operators, themselves, to be in good health and have an abundance of vital elan for the work. We achieved positive results, and in some cases a complete recovery when doctors had given no hope. This was heartening, as much time and effort went into those healing rites.

Gerald asked me to keep him informed of the effects of our magical work and was pleased with our news. I read every worthwhile book on magic and related subjects, and the unseen world opened like a flower and wrapped its petals around me. I had no difficulty in comprehending this new experience I had stepped into. Life was full of wonders.

Both Gerald and I would often have similar dreams, or dreams of which I had one part and he another. It was fascinating to compare notes, and it seemed to us as though we were being informed, or reminded, how the witches of old worked in the Magic Circle. They had different words to express things in those days, and in the dreams these words were accompanied by a recognizable symbol, which at once clarified their meaning. Sometimes, a woman's voice, low and sweet, would discuss a secret aspect of the rituals and emphasize the need for performing them calmly and without haste.

A past witch sometimes came through during a meeting, and still keeps in touch today. Initially, she gave her name and where she had lived, and proceeded to inform us of important aspects of the rites. *She* also used unfamiliar words, but was insistent that we follow her instructions. I told Gerald about this, and he said that he had only recently received similar information in another dream – and, what is more, he was *shown* what was meant. In this way, we were enlightened still further on the old ways of working magic, not least I believe, for our dedication to the Craft and to the Old Gods.

Arnold began to experience visions during sleep, which revealed knowledge at spiritual and karmic levels. As a rule, these occurred at the time of the full moon, and as my husband had Cancer rising in his natal chart, it would seem that he had an especial rapport with that orb.

Time passed, then Gerald informed me and my husband that a further elevation in the Craft would be granted. The Second Degree, or Initiation Proper, took place at Gerald's covenstead on the 11 October 1961, with the Third Degree occurring on 14 October (which just happened to be my birthday, although this was coincidental). Gerald went to a silversmiths in Sheffield and bought a sheet of silver. With this he fashioned one of his now famous magical bracelets for me, and a silver crown with a crescent moon upon it. (Such items of regalia have become popular since Gerald first introduced them into the Craft, but, as he said at the time, it was the *necklace* and the *garter* that were the ancient and traditional insignia of the female witch.) He enjoyed making jewellery, and often endowed it with magical power, in the process. He certainly wrought many beautiful pieces in his time.

Gerald performed a special ceremony and crowned me 'Queen of the Sabbat', an ancient title in the Craft which I will address in a later chapter. As it happened, a reporter turned up the next day, requiring a picture, so we posed, in secular attire, with Gerald holding the crown over my head. Later, this pictorial evidence of the ceremony was to prove fortuitous in confirming that it had indeed taken place.

At Samhain that year, a female journalist requested an interview in which she asked me if I would like to meet more people with similar interests to my own. I said that I would, and the next evening, the *Sheffield Star* headed its report

'Witch seeks recruits for coven' – the antithesis of what I had reiterated about the Craft's unwillingness to procure converts.

In the event, people came to our door, or rang us up, all requesting admittance to the coven. We talked to all reasonable seekers, and eventually initiated our first neophyte, Alan Wharton, who was not only happy to be known as a witch, but was proud to have been the Sheffield Coven's inaugural member. He was closely followed by another male initiate, Vince Davidson, and these two blended well with Arnold's and my own sign of Libra, being Aquarius and Gemini, respectively. In this way, the Sheffield coven came into being – as I always say, purely by accident, or at least without any preconception on our part.

Gerald gave me a rather elegant planchette, and late one evening my mother and I decided to try it out. With letters of the alphabet placed on the table and our fingers lightly touching the planchette we waited quietly for a while, then asked, if a spirit was present, could it please use the letters to communicate. Immediately, the planchette moved and proceeded to spell out words.

We ascertained that our 'visitor' was a Frenchman, called Jacques, who had lived in the sixteenth century. He also told us that he had picked up the English language through travelling widely. It seemed that he had turned his hand to a number of occupations, including a period as a sailor, but the gist of the message, was that he had been present at the Battle of Guinegate.

I had never heard of this battle, and could not pronounce the name, so when Jacques had gone, I rushed to find a book on history, from my library. The first to come to hand was an old one, written as an educational work in a question-and-answer style. I looked through the index not very hopefully, but, lo and behold, I found an entry – 'Guinegate, battle of ', and the page reference. The information read:

Q. Why was the battle of Guinegate called the Battle of the Spurs?
A. Because the French spurred their horses in flight, almost as soon as they came in sight of the English Army (1513).

41

Of course, I had heard of the Battle of the Spurs, which resulted in Francis I meeting King Henry VIII at a place that became known as the Field of the Cloth of Gold, but I had not known the battle's original name, which proclaimed *where* it had occurred and by which the French would know it. Obviously, the more popular name was bestowed upon it by the English.

I tried automatic writing, and one night a lady called to see us who was seriously interested in psychic matters. She joined us in the lounge for a period of meditation, but suddenly I grabbed a piece of paper, and began scribbling feverishly. (With automatic writing, there is no conscious control. You just leave your hand holding the pencil over the paper, so that whoever is communicating can control it.) The message came from someone called Tony who said he had only recently passed away. He wrote, 'Tell Phyl I'm OK and she must go to Ireland as planned. And tell Derrick to buck up, the old sinner.'

I was completely at a loss, as I knew no one in spirit of that name, but Edith, our guest, was extremely excited. She explained that a friend of hers called Phyl had just lost her husband, whose name was Tony. Edith asked if she could ring Phyl at once, and we rushed her to the phone. Once she had got over the shock, her friend was greatly cheered by the message and told Edith that they had planned to go on holiday to Ireland, but her husband's sudden death had made her too unhappy to go anywhere. Edith also relayed the message for 'Derrick'. Had Tony known a Derrick? 'Oh yes,' Phyl replied, 'that was Tony's partner at work – and, do you know, that is exactly how my husband used to talk of him!' So Phyl had received certain proof of life after death, through a personal message delivered via a stranger!

I was invited to Phyl's home, and she showed me a picture of Tony. He was dark-haired and very handsome, and had been only in his mid-forties when he died. It was so strange to see the likeness of someone now in spirit, who had been using my pencil!

The Mysteries were awakening my psychic faculties, and they continued to manifest and grow in a variety of ways. Looking back to childhood, there appeared to have been synchronistic signs – a numinous finger pointing to the future. For example, the time I was the 'Fairy on the Moon' and wore a gold snake bangle (an ancient symbol of the Mysteries); a dance I performed as 'Child Immortal'; the crystal bowl and the prophecy of Madame Melba; and a song I featured, 'In the Valley of the Moon'. There were other things, too. My father's gift of a book entitled *A Masque of May Morning*, and being leading lady in a revue which included a tableau called 'The Legend of the Moon Goddess'. An enthusiastic astrologer looked at my natal chart and exclaimed, 'You have come to blaze a trail in things hidden and mysterious – to champion an old belief and give it new life!' Well, I could not argue with that!

In the Circle, I began to 'see' scenes building up, as though they were on an invisible screen. They were always in lovely astral colours. Arnold teased, 'Just like television – now in colour!'

We were attempting to help a professional gentleman who lived in Southend-on-Sea, and whose business was failing. My clairvoyance, for such it was, showed me a clear picture of him standing at the edge of the sea and contemplating suicide. (Or rather, it was as though *I* was the person on the beach, thinking those thoughts). I rang the gentleman and explained what I had seen, advising him not to do anything silly. He quickly reassured me and said it was during the previous year, in Scotland, that he had stood on the sea-shore and thought of ending his life. So on *that* occasion, the clairvoyance had revealed the past! His business soon improved dramatically, so we put a tick against that problem.

In spite of an increased workload, we still found time to see Gerald fairly regularly. These were precious magical times, in the quiet ambience of Castletown, where the sea laps at the grey stone houses which huddle close to the equally grey castle in their midst. It was the perfect place to unwind and relieve the stresses of living, and Gerald's house in Malew Street, had a marvellous, timeless quality. Add Mrs Jones, the housekeeper, who cooked delicious meals for us, and the situation was complete.

On one occasion, Gerald took us to Douglas. The car arrived, and, as it looked like rain, he pulled a coat from behind the door just before we set off.

Walking round Douglas, Arnold started to chuckle. When I asked what he found so amusing, he said, 'Well, look at Gerald's coat.' I did. It was torn at the back, and the material was hanging down and flapping in the breeze! Gerald exclaimed, 'Oh damn! I picked up the wrong coat. I asked Mrs Jones to throw this one out, but she must have forgotten.' He was quite unperturbed. I happened to be wearing the one smart outfit I had packed, and Arnold, grinning, said 'People will be making remarks, "Look at that woman, all dressed up, and keeping her poor grandfather in rags!" '

Gerald took us down all the back streets, calling in at blacksmiths and ironmongers to collect various bits and pieces, but he bought me a birthday present that day, in the shape of two pairs of shoes! It was very difficult keeping a straight face in the shop, when we saw the assistants staring at that coat! We took Gerald to Castletown's tiny cinema to see *Bell, Book and Candle*, but he fell asleep during the film, just as he did in London when he accompanied us to the Planetarium!

He had a great sense of humour, and one day I asked him if he knew how many books he had. He winked at me, and replied, 'No, dear. But I know when there is one missing!' He was amusing on the telephone, too. He would say, 'Yes, yes,' at intervals, but upon replacing the receiver would mutter, 'Damned if I know who *that* was – couldn't hear a blasted word!'

Our friend told us about an elderly gentleman who had come to the island and whom he knew only vaguely but had invited to dinner. The guest regaled Gerald with the excellence of his pedigree: how he was related to a particular Earl, and a Knight of the Garter just happened to be his great-grandfather. He went on and on in a similar vein, until the end of the meal, when he deigned to enquire into Gerald's ancestry. Did *he* have a distinguished family tree? His host took a sip from his glass of wine, looked the man straight in the eye and said very quietly, 'Well, you know, *Adam* was a gardener!'

Of a letter he received, Gerald commented, 'A man wrote

yesterday saying, "Please send me literature about witchcraft, also send me one of your charms or talismans for Confidence, Love, Health, Romance, Peace of Mind, Courage and Strength, etc: Stamp enclosed, and oblige. P.S. Let me know your remedy for nerve troubles, etc: Please tell me about psychic body and psychic projection".

'I explained I had a museum and had written various books on witchcraft, etc, and gave him prices. I said I did no business in charms, but there were two magazines *Fate* and *Prediction*, which advertised various charms, although I had no knowledge if these were of any use or not. I did not bother to say that I thought there was nothing the matter with his *nerve*!'

In 1962, Gerald Gardner asked us to attend the St Albans covenstead for the Samhain meeting, and this we promised to do. We drove down and located the Fiveacres Sun Club, but not before nightfall. The rain was pelting down in stair-rods as we parked the car in a small clearing just inside the gates.

The surrounding woods looked uninviting and we could not see a proper path to take us to the club-house. Then a light showed, glimmering faintly through the trees, and as it came nearer we saw it was a torch held in the hand of a naked lady! 'I thought I had better come and lead you in,' she smiled. 'It was so much easier coming out like this; my clothes would only have got sopping wet. Now, I can just take a hot shower when we get back.' This was my surprising introduction to Gerald's sun club, or nudist camp, as they were called in the sixties.

There was to be a Fancy Dress dance that evening, which I thought was a hilarious idea for a nudist club. (Perhaps it was the one occasion in the year when they wore clothes. I wondered, idly, if they would recognize each other.) I went as the Queen of Hearts, utilizing a stage dress of white satin embroidered with scarlet hearts. Red satin slippers, and a sweet satin crown, made by Arnold, completed the costume. One lady, with a wonderful tan, was dressed as a South-Sea-island maiden (though perhaps 'dressed' is the wrong word for the tiny flowers, placed strategically upon her person).

Gerald went as a Roman soldier – at least I think that was

the idea; as he had bits of ironmongery fastened to his body, and a sheathed sword which kept getting in everyone's way. I know, because I danced, or rather hopped round the room, with him. Gerald was tone deaf, so we just pranced about, and my shin-bone became a frequent target for his sword. It was quite a relief when the music stopped and it was time for Arnold and I to provide the cabaret.

Later, some of us changed into outdoor clothing, left the party and went out into the woods. We were making our way to Gerald's 'Witch's Cottage' for a meeting of the St Albans coven. The press had got wind of witches' meetings in that neck of the woods, so some witches stood on guard amongst the trees, in case journalists invaded the grounds. An added deterrent came in the form of trip-wires laid in the undergrowth to trap unwary newshounds. We felt perfectly safe to conduct the Samhain rites in peace.

Gerald Gardner bought the cottage from J.S.M. Ward, a friend of his and an author of some repute who ran the Abbey Folk Park, near St Albans. Ward was keen on saving old buildings from being destroyed by local councils, and as a result of his enthusiasm the Folk Park held an outstanding collection. In the course of time, and maybe as a 'thank you' to his friend, for the cottage, Gardner gave Ward and his family his property in Cyprus.

The 'Witch's Cottage' was certainly well preserved, with its whitewashed walls, interspersed with strips of black wood, lattice windows and stout oak door. The interior had been altered to make one large room. Half of it contained an old four-poster bed and a few pieces of furniture, while the remaining space held the traditional nine-foot circle, complete with altar. There was a wonderful atmosphere in the cottage. It was like stepping back in time, and the aroma of incense seemed to permeate the very walls.

It was the first time that Arnold and I had entered the Circle with another coven, but we were warmly welcomed, and the meeting went well. The rites completed, we toasted the Old Gods, then the Circle was closed, and we were soon making our way back to the club-house.

By that time, past two o'clock in the morning, the dance had finished and most of the guests had gone home. Even

Gerald had disappeared with someone who was putting him up for the night. Those who were staying, however, settled down in sleeping-bags, and in the centre of the room a double bed had miraculously appeared! It looked totally incongruous standing in the middle of the dance-floor, and I wondered what on earth it was doing there.

I was very soon enlightened. Jack Bracelin, the High Priest of the St Albans coven and manager of the club, confided, 'That's for you two, as our honoured guests.' I stammered my thanks, and thought, 'How embarrassing!' (I was accustomed to being sky-clad in the Circle, but that was very different from going to bed in a room full of strangers). I changed into my pyjamas in the Ladies Room, then dived into the bed as quickly as I could.

Arnold took it all in his stride, but then he had 'nuded' with Gerald and his friends before. Actually, in the past, he had performed his act for the members of the club. When he told me about this, I asked, 'But where did you conceal your various effects?' (even a brilliant sleight-of-hand magician such as Arnold needed pockets). His reply was amusing, if inaccurate!

I have often wondered if the Witch's Cottage at Fiveacres was still *in situ*. Then, quite recently, a photograph reached me from Australia! The sender, Chris Selwood, spent some time at Fiveacres in his youth and remembers Gerald, Jack Bracelin, Ray Bone and others who were around at that time. Chris tells me that when land was sold off for development the cottage was moved some fifty metres, and it has now become a groundsman's store. Whereas it was once in the middle of a wood, the cottage now stands amidst well-kept lawns and trees and has a new covering of roofing felt, but, he says, still retains 'an amazing "feel" about it'. Near the cottage is a chalet-type hut, decorated with hanging baskets, that his family used to call 'AC', and which still carries the nameplate on the door, 'Ancient Crafts Ltd. Registered Office'.

Since I last saw it over thirty-five years ago, it was quite astonishing to see a photograph of the Witch's Cottage as it is today, and to know that it still exists at Fiveacres Country Club – or, as Chris drily remarks, 'Now, probably only 3½ acres!'

The name of Eleanor (Ray) Bone, stands proud among those High Priestesses who were around in the sixties. She was popular, and did much good work in promulgating the Craft, with appearances on television and radio. Ray also held coven meetings in Gerald's cottage, and was a close friend of Jack Bracelin and Gerald Gardner. Arnold and I were invited to her home in London and celebrated a festival with her people. In this way we experienced the workings of another coven and met new friends.

In her public life, Ray held a responsible position as Matron of a home for the elderly, licensed by the London County Council. When she became an active participant in the Old Religion, she forestalled any gossip that might have arisen from her religious beliefs by informing the leading members of the Council about them personally. Thus she effectually blocked any misconceptions, and also received the assurance that her position in the Craft was a personal matter and would in no way affect her professional standing.

While we were staying with Ray and her husband Bill, a team from the American magazine, *Life International* arrived to take pictures for a feature on the Old Religion. I was included in one of the photographs, and when the article was published we found it to be a most satisfactory and truthful report. Coupled with artistic and atmospheric illustrations, it was a credit to all concerned.

In later years, Ray and Bill retired to Carghill Hall in Cumberland, as she was sick to death of the antics of some so-called witches in London and had no wish to be linked with them. Ray is a most eloquent and capable lady who justifies her title of High Priestess of the Goddess.

3   Secrets from the Past

The Black Book or *Book of Shadows*, as it is known today, was originally a volume containing the secret, magical workings of the Priesthood (that is to say, the coven). It stemmed from an earlier, oral tradition, and from the time when people first began to read and write. Initiated witches are entitled to copy the book and in this way it is handed down.

The rites for the Eight Festivals, or ritual occasions, in the *Book of Shadows* are, however, remarkably short, and Gerald told me that he had written them into the book himself as his parent coven had no such rituals.

I wondered about this, and came to the conclusion that the members of the coven, a chosen body numbering anything up to thirteen souls, were carefully selected people set apart from the populace, and that this discrimination was all-important. The exoteric part of a religion's beliefs are displayed when its followers participate in public rituals, but in most faiths there exists an esoteric nucleus in which certain secret rituals of a magical nature are performed by the priest-hood. This is true of Eastern beliefs, but also of the Old Religion, in which the coven, with its mystical degree system and its conservatism, is nothing more or less than the priest-hood of that religion.

It therefore seems reasonable to suppose that in the olden days, the Festivals of the Old Religion were celebrated chiefly by the *populace*, and were the natural expressions of the people. They were carefree, joyous actions that came from the heart and the group-soul of a particular community: the lighting of boon-fires, maypole dancing, processions and secret assignations in the greenwood.

The Priesthood of the Old Religion may well have officiated in some public rituals, although, as Gerald commented,
these were not part of the coven's magical lore. One can well
imagine the priests and priestesses progressing up the sacred
hill, their path strewn with herbs and flowers, to officiate at
a ritual in the temple. (It was just such temples that the
Christian Church later adopted for its own use, or pulled
down in order to erect its own edifices.)

The coven existed for several important reasons. To work
magic for religious, political and personal goals and, like any
other priesthood, to train the most promising of its members
and ordain them in their turn, so that the knowledge was
passed on. During the witch persecutions in the sixteenth and
seventeenth centuries this priesthood dived underground in
order to survive, but magic was still practised secretly, to try
and lift the persecutions. Because of this dark period in our
history, covens became even more elusive, but witches still
imparted the magical knowledge to their sons and daughters,
or to their Brothers and Sisters of the Art. I, myself, became
a recipient of such knowledge, and it occurred in the
following manner.

On 10 January 1962, Arnold and I appeared on Tyne-Tees
Television in *North East Roundabout*, and Jean, a Scottish
witch, saw the programme while she was staying at the White
Lodge Hotel in Durham. As a result of this, she wrote to me,
the first of many letters.

After a correspondence of several weeks, in the course of
which she requested an oath of secrecy from me, Jean began
to forward rituals from her family tradition. These 'Inner
Rites', as she called them, contained the *symbols* of the Craft
as revealed in the Degrees, and thus disclosed, as Jean
affirmed, that an initiate must have passed through all three
Degrees before receiving them. (However, it would be wrong
to assume that even by this criterion these rituals would automatically be granted. Very often, the Inner Rites would be
handed down within the family via the mother, or the grandmother – the blood ties were often deemed to be the safest).
The way in which the symbols of the Craft are incorporated
into these rites, confirms in no uncertain manner the validity
and structure of the Craft as a continuous, unbroken tradition

50

from the distant past. It was fascinating to see the way in which they revealed a link between the practices of the New Forest coven (passed to me by Gerald Gardner), and those from Jean's family group in Scotland.

One interesting variant of these two sources concerned the names they used, particularly those for the Four Gates of the Circle In Gerald's *Book of Shadows* they are described as the 'Four Quarters', whereas Jean knew them as the 'Four Winds'. In the Western Magical Tradition, East equates with Air and South with Fire; West aligns with Water, while North represents Earth. These descriptions portray the *quality* of the prevailing winds, as they are recognized in the northern hemisphere. The appellation 'Four Winds', also brings to mind the old Gaelic expression for them, namely, the 'Four Airts'.

Before forwarding these rituals, Jean told me that she had performed various divinations on the characters of both Arnold and myself. She was almost certain that my husband was a twin. This, I assured her, was correct.

In order that my reader may understand how Jean regarded the Craft, it is necessary to reveal her thoughts upon it in the closing years of her life. So here are some extracts from her letters. The initial one bore the address: 'White Lodge Hotel, Stanley Road, Durham'.

Dear Mrs Crowther

I was very interested to read about you and your husband in the paper and to see you on TV from Newcastle. I have been a witch all my life and come from a long line of witches as far back as the witch-hunting days.

My ancestors, knowing the old rites, were able to escape death from burning. I say burning because we are Scots, and that was the fate of witches up there.

Although I have been a practising witch, I have never belonged to a coven, working only in the family circle. The rituals were handed down through the years.

I have been interested in the modern revival of the Craft and have read all the books published on the subject. I believe that Mr Gardner knows more of the truth than anybody. But I pray to the Goddess that he will not accept anyone into the

Circle who is unworthy, as it would be so easy to revive the persecutions of the Church.

I noticed, particularly, how you were very cautious to veil the methods of obtaining the power, so I am sending you this rite, as I am a very good judge of character and feel that you are one to help carry on the Craft, and should know everything about it.

As I feel that I may not be long in this life, I don't want any of the old rites lost. You must keep this very secret and only between you and your husband, or others who are as elevated as yourself. Any witch-chant could be used, but here is one written by some past witch for the purpose. When the rite is finished, the Gods must be thanked for their attendance. May you carry on the Craft and have every happiness.

Blessed Be.
Jean.

Dear Mrs Crowther

My sister has come down from Scotland and brought a case of my things, so I am able to send you the athame [black-hilted knife] that I promised you. It belonged to my grandmother, so it should have some power in it . . . I am afraid that it is a bit rusty. I have tried to clean it and polish the handle a bit. It has been consecrated, but a long time ago . . . I am afraid my witch days are about almost over, so I present it to you and hope it will bring you all your wishes and happiness.

I am going to stay in Spain with my sister-in-law, as the weather here is no good for me. They are Catholics, as her second husband was a Catholic, so I will no longer be able to talk about the Craft, but you will be in my thoughts and I hope that you will develop into a powerful witch as my grandmother was.

Blessed Be.
Jean.

My Dear Pat

I have received your letter, just as I was leaving for Scotland. You could write to me c/o the GPO, and if I am not well enough the gardener will collect them.

My friends are very nosy people and will try to find out

who I write to. It wouldn't really matter, but I can't abide such ways of interfering with other people. . . .

P.S. When doing Magic you must get rid of all negative thoughts. You know you can do it and it will work. You can see from the little you have done for me that you are on the right track. Do some every day; Magic is like music, it must be continually practised and it will get stronger every time you do it. . . . I personally don't like covens with lots of people as among so many there must be some negative thoughts that spoil the power. . . .

Dear Pat

I have not written before, because I have been working a lot of magic to try and get the BBC to stop their televising of the ritual. I hope that it will work. It is very wrong to give away the secrets. I feel sure the Goddess will step in to stop it.

I have told you that one must treat the Craft seriously. The Gods will work with you if you keep to the right path that pleases them. It is no easy matter either, to be a High Priestess, she must never err. The ordinary witch can be more easy-going.

I would like you to take my grandmother's place in the Craft. Your picture in the paper reminds me of her when she was young. If you had black hair you would be just like her. You may *be* her, as she must have died long before you were born. I don't want to see the Craft die out and that is why I am sending you this information while I have the opportunity. Please keep it all to yourself. . . . All religions, especially ours, have their Inner Circle and chosen few, I have chosen you to be one of them. . . .

In the above letter, Jean is speaking of a Craft ritual due to be televised at that time, featuring Gerald Gardner and Monique Wilson. In the event, it was in fact condensed and became part of an amalgamation of the usual 'witchy' type of shots and sequences. Jean's magic worked!

Dear Mrs Crowther

I am afraid that illness prevented me going to Spain, but I will be going as soon as possible. My movements are now in other people's hands, so I can't tell you when I shall go. However, I am glad to be spared to be able to write to you again and tell you more about the Craft.

I hope you could read my writing to get the rites going. They may want some sorting out because I burnt my book when I depended on others, not knowing I should ever find a witch to give them to, and have to write it all from memory, so maybe some is missed out, I don't know. Do not let it out of your hands. . . .

It is harder to be a true witch than a Christian! You will find that the Goddess punishes every little error we make. Little things go wrong for us and we suddenly realize that we have done something to betray the perfect trust. It is like the Law of Karma, it never fails.

The Goddess tries to make Her Children pure to work magic for Her and themselves. The powers of Evil are so strong that they can creep in if the witches are off their guard. We are on a dangerous subject.

I have discovered that the Old Gods want to return and realize that they must fight Christianity by suppressing it with good. It could be done, but it is a very hard task. At present, perhaps the Buddhists are the purest religion. That is why the lamas are able to work so much magic. The worldly things have helped to kill our magic in the European countries. It started as the decline when the Magicians used it to try and get gold and riches, and has been going down ever since.

If you try to follow the Goddess, she won't let you starve, and you will soon find things begin to go your way and you get on the up and up. The modern person is too impatient and won't wait for things to work their own way. Just because one becomes a witch one can't expect the Goddess to do things straight away for you. She watches you all the time, and when she is satisfied with you, then she sets things in motion.

You may even get what you think are setbacks, but really these are for your own good. The Goddess will lead you as a mother leads her children.

The Magician broke away as he wanted to command, yet where is he today? Nowhere! The Rosicrucians were a very old mystical school and had great power, but when it was revived in 1909 by the Americans, they needed it to make

54

money, anyone could join if they paid the fees. It is now worthless. So, with most mystical societies. Sex finished Crowley's O.T.O., which could have been really great.

My grandmother never had a coven because she had reached such a high state, she was frightened that others would spoil it for her. I doubt if many true witches were hanged or burnt. Those that were, were just dabblers, in it for gain. The big Sabbaths became commercialized and lost their great power. The persecutions were the punishment of the Goddess. The hideous way the Church carried them out was the beginning of the fall of the Church's power. They failed to follow their leader, Christ, as the witches failed to follow the Goddess.

I hope you understand what I am trying to tell you. Keep on with your magic and worship of the Goddess, and you will see how things begin to act. Don't expect too much at first, and don't be discouraged. I will always be guiding you. You have all my love, my witch daughter.

Blessed Be!
Jean.

The last two letters from Jean were delivered in an extra-ordinary manner. Mother and I went shopping, and when we returned Arnold informed us that he had had a visitor. He explained that a gentleman called who had met Jean at a hotel in Spain, and he presented Arnold with a letter addressed to me. The visitor was a representative for a firm of biscuit-manufacturers, and Jean had asked him if he would deliver a letter to me when he was next in Sheffield, as she had forgotten the number of my house and was anxious for me to receive it.

Seeing a photograph of me, the 'messenger' remarked, 'The lady looked more like a witch than your wife!', and he mentioned that Jean was confined to a wheel-chair and was a very old lady. Unfortunately, Arnold failed to enquire *where* in Spain the gentleman had met her, which made me rather angry with him.

A few weeks later, I found a letter on the door-mat delivered by hand. It was another letter from Jean! Both these letters were inside two envelopes and fastened with lots of

Sellotape. In one of them, Jean explained how she had met the man in her hotel, and felt that she could trust him to bring the letters to me. She had recalled other rituals that she wanted me to have and said they were possibly the last ones she would send.

I never heard from her again, but at the time I thought of the old saying that a witch cannot die until she has passed on her secrets. Now that Jean had discharged her duty to another witch, she was free to become young again, beyond the 'Gates of Death'.

Jean did send me her grandmother's athame – though I marvelled how it managed to reach me. (It was wrapped in brown paper, but the string had come loose, and the ends of the parcel were exposed. How it arrived without slipping from its wrappings I shall never know, but I thank the Gods that it did.) As I held this artefact, that had been so carefully wrought for a Scottish lady all those years ago, I felt privileged indeed to be its new owner. But, was I its new owner? Had I taken possession of an athame that was once mine? The ways of the Goddess are truly miraculous, but there it was, the athame of a High Priestess who had lived more than a hundred years ago!

Many people think that Gerald Gardner obtained the signs on the hilt of the athame from *The Key of Solomon*, a magical grimoire translated and edited by S.L. MacGregor Mathers in the late nineteenth century. However, the signs on the hilt of the athame I received from Jean, although considerably smoothed by constant handling, were identical to the ones on the silver knife which Gerald presented to me at my initiation. As he said at the time, 'This is for now, but I'm sure you will come across a knife with the traditional black handle, in time.' He was right – again!

We must bear in mind that *The Key of Solomon* was not printed until 1888, and, as its author states, 'Save for a curtailed and incomplete copy published in France in the seventeenth century, has never yet been printed, but has for centuries remained in Manuscript form inaccessible to all but the few fortunate scholars to whom the inmost recesses of the great libraries were open.' Are we to believe that the erstwhile owner of my 'new' athame, living in the Scottish

Highlands about 150 years ago, somehow traced the where-abouts of these manuscripts and copied the markings? Now that this much older athame has come to light, this is what Gardner's detractors will have to assume.

Moreover, there are obvious differences between the athame of the witch, and the drawing of 'the knife with the black handle', in *The Key of Solomon*. For instance, there are one or two symbols on witches' athames that are not shown on the drawing, and there are also differences in the shape of the blade: in the drawing the blade is cut away in a curve, an inch from the tip, while those used in the Craft have normal, tapering blades. Conversely, there are characters engraved on the blade in the drawing that do not appear on witches' athames. My own knife departs from the norm, in that the blade has been delicately hammered along the centre in a pattern of tiny, wavy dots which are also echoed on the oppo-site side.

Jean's grandmother was born a witch, her parents being a High Priest and Priestess. In Jean's words, 'This was a wonderful thing for her, as she had lots of power and became very strong in the Art.' Jean's mother eschewed the Craft. She was a regular churchgoer, as was her sister, so Jean was initi-ated by her grandmother and became her 'maiden'. We are looking here at a tradition that goes back two hundred years at least: as Jean said, 'as far back as the witch-hunting days'. So there must surely be other, similar witch-families else-where, in which the Craft and its rituals have also survived.

At the time of Jean's communications I also received important letters from various parts of the United Kingdom and one from the USA. None of the writers disclosed their address, in case the letters went astray, but they all informed me of magical ways of working and worship which each writer felt I should know, if I was not already *au fait* with them. This was quite amazing, because, to judge from the postmarks, they came from totally unrelated sources.

One writer was a lady who said that she and her husband had worked in the Circle with Gerald when he lived in London; her husband had subsequently become headmaster of a school in Wales, and they continued to work magic for the Goddess. Another letter was headed 'c/o the GPO,

Yeovil', and a third, from Glasgow, explained that the writer's grandam had for many years been 'Queen de Sabbat' on Tiree, a very small island in the Outer Hebrides. She said that her grandam had believed that the people who are meant to be instructed and initiated discover the way for themselves. My informant also mentioned that she possessed the athame and cup, and these had belonged to her great-great-grandam, who had passed them down, together with a pentagram-inlaid book support.

Most people understand that witches existed in ancient times, but what seems to raise their hackles is the fact that they also exist in the present day. The late Dr Margaret Murray received much criticism for suggesting that witches were organized in covens and also had leaders – even though her book *The Witch Cult in Western Europe* (1921) included a long list of covens, together with the names of their members, from the sixteenth and seventeenth centuries. Dr Murray made it clear that she believed the witches worshipped the Goddess Diana, but in her second work on the subject, *The God of the Witches* (1933), she emphasized the male deity, as the title suggests. Again, she was vilified, this time by the witches themselves, for supposedly ignoring the Goddess. They seemed to think that the author knew very little about Her. However, I have proof to the contrary.

The Journal of the Royal Anthropological Institute vol. lxiv, 1934, featured a seven-page article by Dr Murray entitled 'Female Fertility Figures'. It carried thirty-two illustrations of the Goddess, many of them extremely ancient, and included representations of the deity in her enigmatic role as 'Sheila-na-Gig'. Murray asserts that the male, or priapic figures have been more carefully investigated than the female – the latter usually being indiscriminately lumped together under the generic term, 'Mother-goddess'. The author realizes that these female figures can be divided into at least three groups, and classifies them: (1) the Universal Mother, or Isis type; (2) the Divine Woman, or Ishtar type; (3) the personified yoni, or Baubo type. She then proceeds to cover the groups and gives an in-depth and authoritative discussion upon each of them.

I had a stroke of luck at my local second-hand bookshop,

when I picked up Margaret Murray's *The Splendour that was Egypt* (1949), and a few months later discovered an even rarer book of hers, *Ancient Egyptian Legends* (1913). In the latter Murray gives legends of the Egyptian gods, including Isis, whom she describes as 'The Great Goddess, the Mistress of Magic, the Speaker of Spells'.

Although I never met Margaret Murray, we both featured in the same article, 'Witches but no Broomsticks', by Richard Whittington-Egan, which appeared in the magazine *Everywoman*, (November 1963). Despite warnings via the 'bush telegraph' that Egan was going to Sheffield 'to get the blonde witch, Patricia Crowther', I found him to be a refined and intelligent person who had obviously studied the subject. His resultant article turned out to be a serious work with the emphasis in the witches' favour. He came to see me two days after interviewing Margaret Murray, who was already on the far side of her hundredth birthday. His conversation with her made interesting reading. This distinguished Egyptologist, and one of the first women dons at London University, reiterated many of the opinions expressed in her books, and then commented, 'It must be the oldest religion in the world. It goes back to the Old Stone Age – and beyond that, to the very beginning of things . . .'. When it appeared, the article was illustrated with three pictures. One of the Stag God from the Trois Frères cave in the Pyrenees, one of myself, and a large photograph of Dr Murray taken on her hundredth birthday.

In the early sixties, Arnold and I co-operated on what was to be my first endeavour as an author, or at least co-author, of a book on witchcraft. In 1964, we received an encouraging letter from Mr Dawes, who owned the *Isle of Man Times* and had become the director of *Fate*, the occult magazine. Arnold was busy working for Granada television, so my mother and I arranged to have a holiday in the Isle of Man. This coincided with the letter we had received from Mr Dawes, in which he asked me to contact him when I arrived.

We stayed with Miss Florence Cowley and her English setter Debbie in the School House, overlooking the sea at Baldrine. Florence, a delightfully friendly lady with many talents, was an artist of no mean order. Her paintings were shown in exhibitions (one of them at the Palace Hotel in

Douglas, which was opened by the Lieutenant-Governor, Sir Peter Stallard) and were also hung in the J.B. Moore's Liverpool Exhibition at the Walker Art Gallery. Miss Cowley always said that Debbie was psychic and inspired many of her paintings, but she too was endowed with clairvoyant abilities and well-known for predicting the future by tasseography. The local press came to see her while I was there, and a picture of Florence reading my tea-cup duly appeared in a Manx paper.

We had great fun, and Florence would fuss over Debbie, then go off to make us something to eat. Mother, greatly daring, would enquire, 'Have you washed your hands, dear?' and our friend would laugh and reply, 'Oh, yes, I'm just doing it, now.' Ever afterwards Florence called my mother 'Wash-your-hands', and in letters would write, 'Give Wash-your-hands my love', or 'How is Wash-your-hands?'

When I rang Mr Dawes he arranged to call at the School House, and at the appointed time a chauffeur-driven Rolls-Royce turned into the drive. Florence came over all unnecessary and pushed me into her lounge, reserved for VIPs, before hastening to the door. I remember Mr Dawes as a tall, dark gentleman, dressed in black, and thought, irreverently, 'Ah, the "Man in Black".' He was a charming, cultivated person with excellent manners, and the most important thing he said, was that he liked to meet the people with whom he did business. He spoke with a French accent, and proffered a gold cigarette case containing expensive-looking cigarettes, whilst we drank coffee from Florence's best bone-china cups. As a result of that tête-à-tête, a contract for *The Witches Speak* was waiting for me when I returned home.

The Irish Sea is notorious for really heavy seas when the weather is bad, and the day we left the island was one of the worst crossings for many years. A passenger was lost overboard from a ferry sailing to the Isle of Man, which gives some idea of the terrible conditions. We should have delayed our departure, but we did not realize just how bad it was going to be. Once on board, we made straight for the bowels of the ship, and there we stayed for the next five hours, lying on couches with the necessary receptacles close at hand. We renewed contact with our last meal, many times over!

Mal de mer is a terrible affliction, but it never troubles me unless a voyage is really bad – and on that day, the seas were mountainous. The ship would judder almost to a standstill, as it was thrown into the immense trough of a wave, only to be heaved up and teeter giddily on top of the next. It was impossible to stand on one's feet for two minutes, together, and hazardous excursions to the heads were made in a ludicrous crab-like fashion, holding on to anything that looked solid enough to support one's weight.

In her lucid moments, my mother reminisced about a similar occasion when she sailed with my father to the Isle of Man. This was long before I was born, when the ferries were much more primitive and everyone sat on benches in the open air and held on to each other for dear life. On *that* day, Mother said, the waves rose in huge walls, high above the ship, as if they were about to smash it to pieces; it must have been terrifying to see all this going on around you.

In this way, I ended yet another visit to my special magical island, where fate, or 'Fate', in the shape of Mr Dawes, had materialized. Gerald had died some months previously, and I missed him more than I could say. Had he known about the meeting with Dawes, I'm sure he would have been pleased. I could almost hear his voice exclaiming, 'Good Oh!'

4 Double, Double . . .

In the 1960s many people on the occult scene scorned Gerald Gardner's association with witchcraft. To my mind, the principal reason for this was ignorance: even genuine occultists had no idea that the Craft still existed. And, of course, after Gerald's death, his enemies had a field day – the dead are unable to defend themselves!

Although today he has been exonerated from false allegations, at the time, they seemed to gather momentum. In 1964, not long after his death, a small magazine about witchcraft appeared, called *Pentagram*. Its founder, a London Press Relations consultant, hid behind the pseudonym of John Math, and the few contributors to its sparse pages likewise adopted *noms de plume*. *Pentagram* was to be the voice of the 'Witchcraft Research Association', the brain child of 'John Math', who hoped to bring Gerald Gardner's initiates together with those other traditions of witchcraft, for the betterment of all concerned.

In fact, the magazine's effect turned out to be the exact opposite of what was intended – if we are to believe its founder. One or two hereditary witches started to air their views in its pages; one, 'Taliesin', proceeded to attack Gerald in a particularly venomous way, and was equally scathing about his followers, whom he named, 'Gardnerians'. This word was coined in order to imply that Gardner's initiates, and those whom they in turn initiated, were *personae non grata*, and that Gerald had never received a genuine initiation. The name Gardnerian stuck, and ever after became synonymous with Gerald's followers – or, more correctly, with those witches immediately descended from him.

One of my initiates used to say, 'Remember the "Old

Contemptibles". Gerald will come out on top, you'll see!' He was right. *Pentagram* soon folded and disappeared without trace, as anything built on sand has a habit of doing, and the hereditary witches were found to be nothing of the kind; one of them had been initiated into the St Albans coven and grown too big for his boots. Always, but always, the Goddess sorts them out! All things considered – not least the fact that Gerald Gardner was instrumental in bringing the Old Religion back into the conscious mind of the race – his name will be remembered with affection long after his old enemies have vanished into obscurity. In Britain, America and elsewhere in the world Gerald's name is already synonymous with the Great Goddess as 'the messenger' who brought the Mother back to Her orphaned children.

Another long-standing enigma must now be aired within these pages. I refer to Alex Sanders and questions surrounding his affiliation to the Craft. Did he achieve a genuine initiation? And if he did, who performed it for him? If he did not, how did the *Book of Shadows* fall into his hands? I feel it is my duty to inform readers of my *first-hand* knowledge of Alex Sanders from the time he contacted me and expressed interest in the Craft of the Wise. There has been much glossing over of Sanders' character by his followers (which to a certain degree is understandable), the fourth estate and, not least, some authors of books on witchcraft. (The latter usually accompany their comments with such qualifications as 'I believe it to be the truth', or 'this is what I believe occurred', to let them off the hook). The Craft, and pagans in general, deserve some straight answers to what has hitherto been shrouded in secrecy or downright invention.

To begin at the beginning, I must go back to 1961, when Arnold and I appeared on Granada television in a news programme, *People & Places*. We were asked to explain our views on witchcraft and, as a result, received many letters from interested viewers. One, dated 9 November 1961, was from an Alex Sanders, who gave his address as 390 Collyhurst Road, Manchester 9. It began:

Dear Mr & Mrs Crowther,
I saw you both on TV, in the *People & Places* programme, and

I was so interested that I have taken the liberty of writing to you. To be a 'witch' is something that I have always wanted – and yet I have never been able to contact anybody who could help me.

Sanders went on to talk of his experiences of second-sight, and thought that this first occurred when he was about twelve years old. His grandmother was telling him about her childhood in Wales, and of how her great-great-grandmother was a witch on Mount Snowdon. He mentioned that he always felt different from other people, and ended the letter by saying he hoped we might be able to advise him. It was signed, 'In all sincereness, Alex Sanders.'

June Johns' biography of Sanders *King of the Witches* (1969) states that he was initiated by his grandmother at the age of seven, and, according to the description of this ritual, it consisted of the young Sanders being nicked in the scrotum with a sharp blade. (It is very difficult to associate such a barbaric act with initiation into the Craft, or indeed anything else, and for a child of seven to undergo such a thing, seems the utmost cruelty.) Immediately, we have a discrepancy. In the letter referred to above, Sanders said that his grandmother *told* him about her forebear who was a witch, and that this occurred when he was not seven but *twelve* years old. He mentioned nothing about an initiation in that letter, nor when he subsequently talked to us.

I answered all the letters I received, including the one from Sanders, and I invited him to come and see me. At the time another Mancunian was interested in the Craft, and he agreed to bring Sanders over in his car.

That I disliked Alex Sanders from the start has never been a secret, so my feelings will not come as a shock to anyone associated with witchcraft. He came to our home on only *three* occasions, and at no time did he set foot in my temple.

The first occasion was on 25 January 1962 and when Sanders and his 'chauffeur' arrived, I introduced him to Alan Wharton, the premier member of the Sheffield coven, who was also present that evening. Later on, someone suggested that we hold a seance, and everyone, including my mother, joined in. But Alex was soon standing up and waving his arms about. He was also spitting what he hoped was ectoplasm into the air. Mother was horrified and left the room at once, but it was obvious that he was putting on an act in the vain hope of impressing us. Sanders was not a success that night.

On his second visit (in the morning of 18 June 1962), he wanted to try the planchette. We obliged, and a spirit calling himself Aleister Crowley came through (we often had messages from Crowley). This time, all he could manage to say was 'Chuck the bugger out!' Sanders enquired, '*What* did he say?', and I contrived to camouflage the awkward moment, by replying, 'I think he said, "It's a lovely day out".'

On that occasion Sanders boasted to us that he could make the front page of the *Manchester Evening Chronicle & News* any time he liked. We were immediately on our guard, and I pointed out that almost anyone could achieve *that* doubtful privilege if they were prepared to perform a stunt of a sensational nature. However, true to his word, what was to be the first of many similar 'witchcraft exposés', appeared on the front page of that newspaper on 15 September 1962, with the headline, 'AMAZING BLACK MAGIC RITES ON CHESHIRE HILLSIDE, Dead Man comes to life, joins witches'.

One of the four photographs illustrating the article showed Sanders kneeling over the 'candidate', who lay swathed like a mummy with a painted mask over his face. Various magical implements covered the candidate's body, and lighted candles were dotted around a circle, outlined with rope. Another picture revealed two reporters and the photographer, Stan Royle, sitting blindfolded at the edge of the circle. (One of the reporters, David Duffy, recorded that 'Before the ceremony, and in order to see what was going on, we had to agree first to be blindfolded.') Apparently, the rite was so secret that none could witness it – apart, that is, from the newspaper's readers! As Arnold remarked, 'If they were all blindfolded, who took the pictures?'

Far from conducting a rite of witchcraft, Sanders was attempting to emulate the 'Opening of the Mouth' ceremony from the Egyptian *Book of the Dead*, and he was holding what looked suspiciously like a pair of chopsticks, with which to open the 'candidate's' mouth!

The report said that Sanders had been a witch for a year, and he told the reporter, David Duffy, that he was going to marry his High Priestess, a thirty-two-year-old woman from Nottingham. Sanders had moved quickly in the space of a few months, not only had he met another High Priestess, he was going to marry her.

A painting of the Moon Goddess appeared in the article's main photograph, just behind the 'candidate's' head. In her book, *The Rebirth of Witchcraft* (1989) Doreen Valiente says that she immediately recognized it as the work of Arnold Crowther and wondered how it had come to turn up there. The answer is very simple. At that time Arnold painted lots of pictures, and the Mancunian who had initially brought Sanders over to see us offered to take some of them, including the painting of the Goddess, and try to sell them for my husband; it was quite obvious to us that Sanders had borrowed that particular painting to add authenticity to the 'rite'. Arnold was none too pleased about it, as it was never returned, and he received no payment for it. (In point of fact, two of Arnold's paintings were used in those photographs, the other being that of an Egyptian mummy which was propped up at the feet of the 'corpse'.)

About this time, Gerald Gardner received a letter which he duly forwarded on to me, from a woman who lived in Nottinghamshire. It expressed the writer's desire to enter the Craft, so we arranged to meet her, and eventually she was initiated into the Sheffield coven. So now, with the exception of Arnold and myself, all the initiates were working in the First Degree of the Craft. It is commonly assumed within the Craft that a female initiate left the Sheffield coven to form one of her own, and that Alex Sanders was initiated into that coven. But the important thing here is that this person did not have the necessary qualifications or knowledge to form her own coven – i.e. she was not a High Priestess. It was not until the 1970s that a female member of the Sheffield coven achieved this status and started a new group. (Before that time some male witches successfully branched off, one of them initiating his fiancee and founding a coven in Scotland. At least five further covens evolved from that one.)

On the 28 June 1962, one of our female initiates called to see us, and soon afterwards Alex Sanders also arrived on what proved to be his third and final visit. My two guests met each other and in my presence exchanged addresses and telephone numbers. On 27 August 1963 Gerald Gardner, who used to say that he heard things on the 'jungle telegraph' received a curious letter from Sanders which he forwarded to me. In this letter, Sanders said that he was invited to visit a witch whom he had met at my house, to explain a misunderstanding concerning the person's supposed part in his recent publicity, and that after the matter was cleared up his visit was prolonged for several days. He then went on to say that during his stay he met a High Priestess from Derbyshire, called Medea, and asked her to initiate him. She apparently agreed, as Sanders then states that the rite was performed on 9 March 1963. He also says that on this same occasion his hostess was made a High Priestess! (But by whom? There is no mention of a High Priest being present.) Another letter on the same issue was written to Gerald on 5 September 1963 and a copy of it is in my possession. (This was one of the many letters which formed part of Gerald's estate, later sold to Ripley's; eventually, Ripley's sold all the papers and documents, and they are now privately owned but available to leaders of the Craft to view and/or copy.)

The letters referred to here were written within a period of nine days, and were more or less saying the same thing: that someone called 'Medea' initiated Sanders after meeting him for the first time.

However, a little earlier in 1963 (on 8 June to be precise) Gerald received a letter from someone who lived in the Midlands and who signed himself 'Vulcan'. This letter was also forwarded to me. The writer explains that he has been interested in magic and witchcraft for a very long time and gives chants and prayers, mostly taken from published sources. He then says that he met a woman at a Spiritualist lodge who said she was a witch. She told him what witches do and believe in, as far as her oath allowed, and said that her witch name was 'Medea'. Vulcan states that he met her many times, but on 12 January that year (1963) she died at the age of sixty-two.

Now, although we know that the writers of the first two letters were talking about a witch called Medea, who was initiating people, *including those of her own sex*, in March 1963, Vulcan's letter says that she died on 12 January in that year! It must therefore be assumed either that Medea was initiating folk in her astral body, or that there were two High Priestesses with the same witch name from the same area (which is highly unlikely).

It was also very unusual for Gardner to receive *three* letters within the space of seven months, all talking about a Medea – a fairly uncommon witch name. Uncommon, yes, but (apart from the murderess of that name in Greek myth) I do recall seeing it once before. In *King of the Witches* June Johns tells us that Sanders' grandmother, who died during World War II, had the witch name of Medea.

It has also been suggested that Alex Sanders went to see Gerald Gardner, and that Gardner offered him the *Book of Shadows* to write out. Nothing could be further from the truth. On reading Sanders' sensational press stories, Gerald was horrified and commented to me, 'He'd better not come here – I don't want to be mixed up in anything to do with him. Sanders had better watch out. If he shows up he'll get the "Order of the Boot"!' In no circumstances would Gerald Gardner have offered Sanders the *Book of Shadows* to copy out. The idea is ludicrous. And if Sanders had achieved a proper initiation, it follows that he would have copied parts of the book, in the usual manner of initiates.

A story went the rounds at that time that Alex was going to introduce Gardner at one of his gatherings. Gerald heard about this and was highly amused, he said, 'Now, I wonder, is Sanders going to get someone with a white beard and introduce him as Gardner? Of course, the impostor would have to have both forearms tattooed, also a small dagger on his left upper arm and a pixie dancing on his left leg. My right thumb has had a bullet through it, and I have only a sort of claw instead of a nail on it. All this would have to be copied to make for a good impostor; I don't think he will be too happy about it!'

As for the *Book of Shadows*, I happen to know how, and from whom, Sanders obtained a copy of it. One of the

68

witches concerned lives on the Isle of Man to this day, but wishes to remain anonymous (primarily because of his particular circle of friends and associates). Since I have promised to keep his confidence, I will refer to him as 'Fian'.

We occasionally took friends and/or initiates to the Isle of Man to meet Gerald Gardner (with his prior permission, of course!), and there was usually an invitation to have dinner with Fian and his wife, who were members of Gerald's coven. These were very merry evenings spent with charming people, and, as always, I was happy and relaxed in Gerald's company. The Craft meetings, especially, were occasions which I will never forget. After one of these magical holidays, however, the unforeseen and unthinkable occurred. Fian rang me out of the blue, sounding extremely perturbed. I managed to calm him a little, but I was totally unable to believe what he was saying.

Apparently, one of the witches we had taken to the island had returned there and turned up on Fian's doorstep. Neither Fian nor his wife could believe their eyes but, being civilized folk, they asked him in and enquired what had precipitated his sudden reappearance so soon after returning to the mainland. The visitor said he had returned to ask Fian if he could borrow his *Book of Shadows* to copy out; he assured him that he would keep it safe and send it back within a week. Fian told me that he thought the chap was *bona fide* as *we* had taken him to see Gerald (sadly, we had thought so, too), so he did indeed lend the book. He was now ringing me because it had not been returned! Fian grumbled that the witch had had it for three weeks and could I ask him to send it back, at once?

I was at a complete loss for words. I felt betrayed, angry – but at the same time incapable of realizing such a thing had happened. I was also dismayed by Fian's actions; surely he had known that the book should not have left his hands? Gerald would have to be informed, too. I felt shattered.

I rang the witch concerned to ask him what on earth was going on, and to send the book back, immediately. He agreed to return it, but would answer none of my questions. However, when I had talked it all over with Arnold, we both came to the conclusion that Fian's book had passed into the hands of a third party. This was how Alex Sanders obtained the *Book of Shadows*, and why his witchcraft rituals were almost identical to those in the original book.

Sanders had regularly approached covens with a view to being accepted, but apparently had no success. Who can wonder at this? He was already becoming notorious for his bizarre behaviour, and highly inflammatory articles that appeared *ad nauseam* in the press, which brought the Craft of the Wise into disrepute. Some witches said it was Sanders' way of getting his own back on those who had refused him initiation, and this may well be the truth of the matter.

I remembered that Gerald had gone abroad again, soon after we had left the Isle of Man. He contacted me and said, 'I'm just off to Majorca for two or three months. At least, I'm going off with Idries Shah – Majorca first stop. When you go with him you never know where you will end up. He writes on Magic, and he always tries to do the flying-carpet trick – this, when we're getting out of England! He does not like the cold, or I would say, don't be surprised if we tumble down your chimney on Xmas Day!' It was therefore some time before I was able to speak to Gerald about what had occurred. I was certainly not going to worry him while he was away. A letter arrived from a hotel in Malaga, in which Gerald said they had been to see Robert Graves who had given them a very good time. (This meeting with Graves has been documented in two biographies, *Robert Graves and the White Goddess*, by Richard Perceval Graves, and Miranda Seymour's *Robert Graves – Life on the Edge*). Robert Graves, Idries Shah and Gerald Gardner were together for an entire day and renewed their conversations the next day at Canellun, Graves' house in Deyá.

I waited until Gerald came to visit us – what was fated to be our last meeting – then told him the whole sad story. I knew he was not well, so I tried to let him down gently, and apologized for being the bearer of ill tidings. Gerald said it was very bad – very bad indeed, but some people *did* do beastly things. He commented that he would never have believed such a thing of Fian; it was totally out of character. I agreed with that. Our friend looked very frail so we made light of the matter and turned the conversation to happier things, but quite suddenly Gerald's eyes gleamed fiercely and he barked, 'You know, if I had caught that blackguard with the book, I would have let him have both barrels of one of my guns!'

As I explained in *Lid off the Cauldron*, we took Gerald to the Manchester Ship Canal, where he boarded the vessel that was to take him out of our lives for ever. And yet this proved to be true only in a physical sense, for he has often communicated with us from the World of Spirit.

As if to substantiate our opinions in the matter of the *Book of Shadows*, quite a homely gentleman from Manchester called to see us in an extremely agitated frame of mind. When his story came out it appeared that, after meeting Sanders, the latter initiated him, wearing a long white gown, in a so-called Egyptian ceremony which lasted for three hours. It was transparently obvious that this gentleman was devoted to the Goddess and Her Mysteries and was quite genuinely upset when he realized that the ceremony had nothing to do with the Craft of the Wise.

According to our visitor, he was obliged to pay Sanders in advance in order to procure for him certain magical artefacts. He was then presented with an old glass inkwell (in which to keep his oil); a brass cigarette case for the salt and some other bits of rubbish. He brought them to show us, along with his *Book of Shadows* which he had copied from Sanders' book. There was a showdown when he realized he had been taken for a ride.

The writings in this latest *Book of Shadows* were the same as those in the original, apart from one important exception. There, in black and white, was a description of a particular spell, entitled 'Ancient Candle Spell', with an accompanying verse, which was definitely *not* part of the traditional book. This candle spell had come through to me from a discarnate witch during a rite held some months previously. At the time, we were also informed how to work the spell, and Arnold wrote a short verse for it. Apart from Arnold and myself, there was only one other member of the Sheffield coven present that night, and we had agreed to his copying it down *for his own private use*. Seeing this spell together with Arnold's verse, in a copy of Sanders' *Book of Shadows* was a shock, but it certainly confirmed many of our previous fears.

71

Jack Bracelin, the High Priest of the St Albans coven, and Eleanor (Ray) Bone, the High Priestess of the Balham coven, London, were determined to confront Alex Sanders with the matter of his defamatory publicity, and try to make him see some sense. They drove from London to Manchester, calling to put me 'in the picture', on the way. When they arrived at the terraced house where Sanders was living there was no one at home, so they waited in the car for two hours, until he finally put in an appearance. He asked them in, but after listening to their remonstrations he announced that he intended to continue giving similar interviews to the press and anyone else who cared to listen to him. Sanders was totally unrepentant and not in the least abashed by his actions. Nor was he in the slightest way concerned about the adverse effects they were having upon the Craft and its adherents.

Ray said, 'Oh come along! How can you possibly put all this rubbish in the papers about a "Witches' Wedding" when there is no such thing?' Sanders' rather ineffectual reply was that he had only put it in the papers to show what it would be like, if there was such a thing. His 'wedding' was offensive to the witches because newspaper reports described a 'hand-fasting' ceremony photographed in the Circle itself! This ancient rite has no connections with the Christian form of marriage. (And, for the record, my own much publicized marriage to Arnold Crowther some years before bore no comparison. It was a *civil* ceremony conducted in a registry office, and I make no apologies for it).

Sanders was still pursuing his sensational activities in the 1970s, when he attempted to enter the world of the theatre. On 24 January 1971 he was booked at the Classic Cinema in Hendon to present a witchcraft ritual aimed at invoking the demon, Asmodeus. The show was scheduled as a midnight attraction, but things went drastically wrong. On stage, the candle-shaped bulbs round the circle were to be lit on cue, but when Alex went to 'light' the North 'candle', the one in the South was switched on; apparently, everything went downhill from that point. Asmodeus, the demon of anger, failed to materialize (a spectator in the audience later commented that the only suggestion of his presence was when the people demanded their money back at the box office). In spite of this humiliation, Sanders continued with his charade at a night-club in Weston-super-Mare. But, when some men from the audience decided to join in the fun, the resultant fracas was such that the manager cancelled the contract, forthwith.

A few months later, however, two advertisements appeared in the *Sheffield Star*. The first read, 'Civic Theatre, Barnsley, Alex Sanders, "King of the Witches". Dare you meet this man? Sensational attraction, one performance only, March 13th, 7.30 p.m.' Immediately underneath, a second announcement ran, 'Interested in witchcraft? See Alex Sanders, the World's Greatest White Witch – at the Barnsley Civic this Saturday.' The *Sheffield Morning Telegraph*, on the other hand, featured an article, headed, 'Fresh bid to ban witchcraft show', and reported that the Barnsley Town Council were holding a meeting with a view to banning the performance. Councillor Gordon Jepson was quoted as saying 'I have been told that warning notices will be put up in the hall before the performance, but I still think there is a real danger that someone will get injured.' Sanders' agents, Vincent Shaw Associates, claimed that 'the show – which caused a council row at Weston-super-Mare – *can* be dangerous. At one point the witches call on the devil to appear in the magic circle.'

When was all this balderdash going to end? How on earth could a few gestures and incantations be considered as a professional act? It was absurd and, once again, reflected badly upon the Craft.

Then, out of the blue, I received a telephone call from one of the Barnsley councillors, who said he had heard that I was something of an authority on witchcraft. Would I go over and discuss the matter of the witchcraft show with them? I agreed, and a meeting was arranged, a few days before the performance.

Ten councillors were present, and Arnold and I talked to them for a considerable time, answering their many questions. Of course, we realized that these gentlemen knew next to nothing about the subject, and many of them thought we worshipped the devil. We corrected them on this score and we reiterated that what Alex Sanders professed to call witch-craft was nothing of the kind. We objected as much as they did to the staging of such a show; the entire concept was abhorrent to us.

They listened intently to all we had to say, and I believe they were a little more enlightened when we took our leave. However, they did not seem to think the show could be banned at such short notice, because contracts between the agents and the civic authorities had been signed. They were afraid of being sued for breach of contract if they banned the performance at that late stage which made us wonder why they had bothered to contact us at all. So the show went ahead, but it played to only seven people – I was *not* one of them!

It came to my knowledge that certain people were circulating the rumour that Patricia Crowther had initiated Sanders into the Craft. In order to rectify this false allegation I wrote suitable letters to various occult magazines, making it very clear that I had done no such thing. I also contacted Alan Wharton, the first initiate of the Sheffield coven, who had met Alex Sanders at my home. He gave me full permission to publish his name and commented, 'I am proud to be known as an adherent of the Craft.' (Alan was with us for nearly six years before his profession took him abroad to various parts of the world. In this way he was able to contact other covens and groups, and frequently attended their meetings as a guest.) Alan wrote to various pagan publications about the rumour, but the editor of *The Wiccan*, a journal of the Old Religion, declined to print his letter, saying that it would be placed in their archives. With Alan's permission, I therefore include it here:

Dear Sir or Madam,
As a founder-member of the Sheffield coven I must object to the rumour currently in vogue, that the late Mr Alex Sanders was initiated as a member of our coven. That is not true!

Patricia Crowther's coven was formed in November 1961, and I was the first person to be initiated into it. Mr Sanders came to our covenstead three times for assessment, but was not initiated. We questioned his mental attitude, and our conclusion was that he was totally confused in his understanding of the Craft. For this and other reasons, his request was turned down.

A few years later, I saw Sanders again in Leeds where he was attempting to give a talk on witchcraft. In this talk he stated that he was made a member of the Sheffield coven. I challenged him on this, and he said, 'No, not Sheffield, I mean Chesterfield.' I replied that there was no coven operating in Chesterfield at that time. Further, I pointed out that I had met him at Mrs Crowther's home. I said, 'You know me. I met you there.'

Sanders blustered, then publicly stated that he had never met Mrs Crowther, and that he had never been in my company! At this point, I realized that our opinion of him had indeed been an accurate one, and I announced to the assembly that in my opinion, he was a menace to the Craft, if not to society as a whole. I said that he had no true knowledge of the Occult, and that he created more damage to the Craft of the Wise, than any person I had known. With that, he quickly left the hall, and I did not see him again.

Yours faithfully,
Alan Wharton,
High Priest of Wicca.

Sanders' lecture in Leeds occurred soon after the publication of June Johns' *King of the Witches*, and was no doubt part of the promotional campaign that attended it. There is, of course, no such title as 'King of the Witches', and when they heard about it, most witches laughed their socks off. A witch friend of mine declared that the only ruler *she* recognized was the one who lived in Buckingham Palace. A fair comment! Fanciful and silly titles such as these, only bring derision upon the Old Religion, because in the eyes of the general public, they belong to the realms of fantasy and fairy-tales.

In ancient times, a High Priestess would sometimes be given the title 'Queen of the Sabbat', but she was not considered to be a ruler of the witches. Gerald Gardner bestowed this title upon me because he considered that I deserved it, having worked hard to promote the Craft and helped to form covens other than my own.

75

In the realms of witchcraft Alex Sanders certainly succeeded in becoming a controversial figure, so much so that, for good or ill, his adventures will be a talking point for years to come. In the final analysis, however, his friends and the people who knew him best, must be the ones to evaluate his true character.

5   I Psy . . .

In the years that followed my initiation into the Craft, many strange things occurred in the realms of the esoteric. On the whole, these were quite amazing and uplifting, and I welcomed them as part of my development. It was clear that initiation, *per se*, affected all aspects of the individual – physical, mental and spiritual – and, for me, the opening of the 'Third Eye' meant that the veil between the worlds became less opaque. This chapter, therefore, includes a variety of preternatural events, of varying degrees of importance, that it was my fortune to experience.

A small but nevertheless intriguing happening manifested when Arnold and I gave a show at Crewe Hall in Cheshire. A large room in the mansion was put at our disposal, and while preparing for the entertainment we heard a loud 'plop' at the far end of the room. Upon investigation, I found a round piece of carved wood floating in the water of a fire-bucket, with the water still agitated from the impact. The wood was part of the ornate panelling on the walls, and the place it had fallen from was clearly noticeable. However, it was nowhere near the bucket, so the wood could not have dropped directly into the water. We were told that the house had a ghost which often did queer things!

A very special psychic experience occurred at the dentist's. I had discovered an absolutely brilliant dental surgeon in Roy Taylor, who put his patients completely at ease. I was to have a wisdom tooth extracted, but when I arrived, I learned that Roy was on holiday, and someone else was 'filling in' for him. I dithered, thinking I would rather wait until Roy returned, then I had a burst of courage and, thinking, 'What the heck!', sailed upstairs to the surgery.

I expected to be given a gas anaesthetic (in those days an injection of pentathol was unheard of, although Roy was to incorporate it into his work later on) and for some reason, as the mask was put over my face, I decided to examine the effects of being 'put under', instead of succumbing to the anaesthetic as on previous occasions. I did not intend to resist it, merely to examine mentally the sensations of the operation.

The first thing I noticed was an unpleasant tightening in the region of the head: a squeezing, constricting sensation. I knew no more after that until I suddenly felt excruciating agony as the tooth was drawn. It was as though I was wide awake and having the extraction without the gas! While I was 'screaming' inside, there was a 'pop', and I plummeted into dark space where stars shone brilliantly around me. I knew without any doubt, that I had separated from my body, and that this phenomenon was the result of the agony.

I experienced a feeling of spiritual ecstasy; I *was* this ecstasy, it was part of me – I know no other way to describe it. Then, across the dark sky of what I presumed was outer space, or even inner space, a word gradually formed – a word composed of many letters that stretched across my field of vision. And I was able to comprehend that enormous word. It informed me about the meaning of life: of nature, of the animals and of the universe. I thought, 'How wonderful! It is all so very simple, and yet humanity has so many complex theories to explain it.'

The word vanished, and I was still in bliss when a voice spoke from that star-spangled darkness – a beautiful, modulated voice, embracing the utmost compassion. (Whether it was a male or a female voice, I could not discern; perhaps it was neither, at least as we understand voices on Earth.) It said, 'You must go back, now', and I so wanted to stay there for ever in that ecstasy. The words were repeated, 'You must go back, now', and I thought, 'I don't want to go back.' I remembered my dear ones on Earth, but I desired to be part of that rapture, always. Apparently, that was not allowed, as the same words were uttered again, and at last the scene dimmed, and someone was shaking my arm – hard!

I opened my eyes in the surgery, with the dentist's assistant peering at me anxiously. 'We thought you were never going to wake up,' she said. Arriving at the bottom of the stairs, minus a tooth and as high as a kite, I talked excitedly to Arnold as he led me to the car. (I had to return to the dentist's a few hours later, as I was haemorrhaging badly. As Arnold jokingly remarked, I had to have the cavity hem-stitched – it was no joke at the time, though!)

I had no difficulty in coming to terms with the out-of-the-body experience, but I wondered how I could have felt the pain of the tooth being drawn, while I was 'out', unless it had something to do with that conscious effort of mental examination while inhaling the gas. I suppose this could have had something to do with it, but I believe it was actually *feeling* the pain, that shot me out of the body.

I was curious to know where I had manifested. The Manasic Plane is said to be the Plane of pure bliss, so it might have been that State of Being. When I met the occultist and author William Gray, I told him about it, and the word I had seen and understood. He exclaimed, 'Oh, that was the unpronounceable Word of God – the Universal Utterance. You should have kept hold of it, and remembered it.'

I had explained to Bill that after the occurrence, I would dream that I was about to recall the meaning of the word again, but, as I thought I had seen it by chance, it was not meant for me to know it. Hence, I would wake up bathed in perspiration, on the brink of remembering it. I am content, though, to know that it remains hidden in my subconscious mind. Bill also commented that, if I had seen other souls on that Plane, I would not have returned to the body!

Then, there was the matter of the voice. It could have been one of the Guardians, who are said to guide souls back to their bodies if they are thrust out, accidentally, or if it is not their true time to leave the Earth. It could also have been my own higher self (known to cabbalists as the HGA, or Holy Guardian Angel), which among other things guides the soul in life.

Since I entered the Mysteries of the Goddess, I have learned something of after-life conditions. The Ancient Wisdom teaches that there are many 'States of Being', and these are known as the Inner Planes. They are composed of the ethereal qualities of Water, Air and Fire, and in *that* order, from the Earth Plane.

If human beings have physical, etheric, astral and spirit forms, there is no reason to doubt that the elements, from which our bodies are made, also contain these finer properties. They occupy Inner Space, and are set within each other. A good analogy is that of an onion, with its many layers of skins. Some people are unable to comprehend anything they cannot see with the physical eyes. My usual reply is, 'Well, you cannot see *air*, yet it is a very dense gas which we breathe all the time – it keeps us alive! So, how much finer are these subtle Planes that are likewise invisible?'

The people who attend my talks are extremely interested in what happens after death, so I tell them what I have learned through the Old Religion. At the death of the body, and after the usual three days of sleep, there is what is known as the Second Death.

Most souls awaken in their Astral Bodies upon the Astral Plane, the Plane of Emotions. This is composed of the Inner dimensions of Water, has seven divisions and is the one nearest to the Earth Plane. Here, wrapped in its Astral Body, the soul goes through a period of retrospection and contemplates the actions of its last incarnation.

Finer than the Astral, is the Manasic or Mental Plane – the Inner content of Air. Manifesting on this Plane, the soul has discarded its Astral Body (which, much like the physical body, is absorbed by its own element). Here the soul exists as pure thought, but experience of this Plane depends upon the *refinement* of the soul – on whether during its many lives on Earth it has reached the necessary purity, for the Manasic Plane is one of bliss. It equates with the Summerland of the Pagans, the Heaven world of the Christians, the Buddhists' Nirvana and most religious ideas of paradise. This Plane is the soul's true home and is known as the Shining Land, or Land of the Gods. The joy and ecstasy it enshrines is beyond description.

More subtle than the Mental Plane, is the Plane of Godhood: that of Inner Fire. The ancient mysteries inform us of the Teachers – avatars and initiates of all faiths and religions who dwell upon it. These mighty Beings have cast off the fetters of earthly existence; having *earned* this entitlement, and of their own free will, they incarnate upon the Earth solely for the benefit of Humanity.

I believe that these Planes are merely a tiny part of the Whole, which, as we approach it, through many lifetimes, brings us closer to Truth. Each and every one of us is a spark from a Supreme Source of Light. Call it what you will.

After seeing an apparition, many people say that the vision was clothed in light, or was made of light. This would indicate that the soul has risen to the higher Planes. Other spirits are clothed in a grey or dark-hued substance, revealing they have recently passed over, and/or that their present State of Being is that of the Astral Plane.

Raymond, a member of my coven, experienced something uncanny a few weeks before hearing of me for the first time. He would go for long walks on moonlit nights to commune with the ancient Goddess of Nature; he had felt drawn to the Old Gods for a long time, but knew of no one to aid him in his quest. One night, while walking along a high ridge, he stopped to look down. The valley was bathed in the silvery light of a full moon, and far below he could see figures dancing round a fire. The only clothing they wore was the skins of animals, and their shouts and cries could be clearly heard in the stillness of the night, as they raised their arms to the white face of Lady Moon. Raymond knew that he was witnessing a scene of long ago, when our ancestors paid homage to the Goddess of the Moon. He lifted his eyes to the shining orb, and when he looked down again, there was nothing but the silent valley and the sound of an owl hooting in the distance.

When he saw my name mentioned in a newspaper, Raymond wrote to me forthwith. He believed that the Goddess had been showing him the ways of his forebears on that moonlit night – and subsequently led him back to Her worship. Raymond has long been a strong and trusted friend who can be relied upon in any eventuality.

Our work took Arnold and me to many different parts of Britain, and on two occasions, we played the city of Bath. Barry, the person who looked after us during our time there, had been born in Sheffield, and when he was not attending to the needs of the artistes, his duties lay in the museum and the buildings which surround the Roman Baths. It was also his responsibility to make sure the place was secure when the Baths closed for the night.

Barry knew the history of the Baths and recognized that, long before the Romans invaded Britain, the waters had been sacred to the goddess Sulis. On warm, balmy evenings, when everyone had gone, he would often bathe in the hot waters of the King's Bath, and he asked us if we would like to do the same. So, one night, with the stars winking overhead and the vapour from the bath rising to greet them, we walked down stone steps and into the steaming water.

It was a truly amazing experience as we luxuriated in the hot, comforting element, with the Sacred Spring close by. Unlike Arnold and Barry, who could swim, I splashed about, sometimes holding one of the iron rings set in the walls (these rings were installed long ago, when ladies, dressed in their petticoats, bathed in the healing waters). King Charles II, after whom the King's Bath is named, had a stone seat placed on one of its walls, where he could take the waters at his ease. I took the opportunity to sit on the seat which had once held a royal bottom. On our return visit to Bath the following year we bathed on two separate occasions, making the magical three times in all. We regarded these immersions as a true baptism, cementing our allegiance to the Goddess. A privilege, indeed!

Thinking back, I remembered a message we received in the Circle some time previously. It had been short and to the point:- 'Seek the Stone Sun God's disc', and there, overlooking the King's Bath, was the carved stone head of the Celtic Sun God, with another carved head of the Moon Goddess, Sulis Minerva, close by! The Goddess is framed in lunar crescents and holds a flail or whip.

The head of the Sun God has always been referred to as the 'Gorgon's Head', despite the obvious male attributes of moustache and beard. This glaring error was corrected by R.J. Stewart in his book, *The Waters of the Gap* (Bath City Council 1981) (although the erroneous caption still appears on merchandise in the museum shop). The carving, with its flaming aureole of hair and wings is the epitome of the all-seeing, all-hearing God of Light. The god's features are awesome, the ecstatic expression and innate vigour being dramatically captured. The wreath of oak leaves surrounding the head, betrays victory over darkness and vividly expresses the principle of kingship. Both the Celts and the Romans acknowledged the oak as a magical tree, and one associated with the God of the Sun.

Twenty years later, I again went to Bath, this time on holiday. The water level in the King's Bath had been lowered, and a copper-coloured line revealed its original height. Further excavation had revealed huge underground rooms and the broad steps leading to the temple of Sulis Minerva. Various altars of diverse shapes and sizes were also on view, together with maps and plans showing the immense scale of the temple and forecourts. The stone heads of both the Sun God and the Moon Goddess had been moved to this newly excavated site and to even greater advantage.

The 'Waters of the Gap' continue to flow from the russet-stained stones: a boiling, life-giving liquid emanating from the depths of the earth. These waters have drawn people since ancient times. Initially, a few humble huts were raised near the spring; later on Celtic and Roman settlements grew up, and the temple, baths and other buildings were erected. Today a city has grown round the sacred site, and the waters can be taken in the genteel atmosphere of the Pump Room that looks over the King's Bath. These environs contain evidence of many successive phases which have merged over the centuries to provide a most hallowed centre for healing, therapy and worship.

Other cities and towns are not as gracious as Bath, but magical phenomena can occur almost anywhere, I have discovered. Once, when we were working in the Grimsby/Cleethorpes area of the east coast, Arnold and I had arranged to return home after our last date, a children's show. For two days a blanket of fog had covered the district, making driving extremely hazardous, and it looked as though it would be foolish to attempt the journey. However, I desired to sleep in my own bed that night, so I decided to invoke the powers of the god, Odin, and request a strong wind to clear the fog. (The film, *The Vikings* came to mind, in which an old seer invokes this god with a similar request in order to save the life of a young Viking, played by Tony Curtis, who had been tied to a post in a pool, where the water was rising rapidly. The seer cried, 'Odin! Odin! Send a wind to turn the tide – Odin!', or something like that.) We were on the east coast, facing Odin's territory across the North Sea, so I stood on the deserted beach, performed an invocation, and kept the request firmly in mind throughout the day.

The forecast was not good, and there was no mention of a change in the weather, but we performed our show for the children, packed up, and left. Outside it was pitch-black, but in the lamp-light one could see the fog moving and curling, and I felt a cold breeze on my face. We decided to attempt the journey, and Arnold said we could always find somewhere to stay for the night, if the weather failed to improve. The head-lights of the car revealed swirls of fog being shifted into fantastic shapes – a wind was picking up! Driving through open country we could see some way ahead, as the now strong wind whipped around our vehicle.

We stopped at a road-side inn for a non-alcoholic drink, and the proprietor enquired where we had come from. 'Grimsby,' we replied, in unison. 'And that doesn't mean we want a *small port*!', I added. The bartender grinned, then exclaimed, 'But, the fog's been terrible there. They said you could not see a hand in front of you!' We agreed it had been pretty bad. 'It's funny,' he remarked, 'only a couple of hours ago it was bad here, then a wind blew up and started to shift it. Funny old weather, 'aint it?' We said that it was, thanked him, and left. Outside, I poured the contents of the miniature bottle of brandy I had bought on to the grass. After all, only the best was good enough for Odin.

During our travels, we met many interesting people, some of whom were occultists, themselves. There was William Gray, and his wife, Roberta (Bobbie), whom we first met at Doreen Valiente's home. For many years, after seasons spent on the south coast, the Grays invited us to stay with them on our way back to Sheffield. This was always towards the end of September, and it came as a welcome respite after a hectic working period. We dived eagerly into the much-needed esoteric atmosphere of the Grays' home in Cheltenham and regularly enacted the Autumn Seasonal Ritual. It was a joy to work with these experienced ritualists.

The ceremony was one of four from Bill Gray's *Seasonal Occult Rituals*, which as the title suggests encompasses rites

84

for the four seasons, each one in harmony with a particular time of the year. When this book was first published, in 1970, it was said that the rites were too pagan for the Christians, and too Christian for the pagans. In fact, the rituals are universal, and one has only to adapt a word here and there to satisfy the pedant.

Bill was a fascinating character and well schooled in magic and the Cabbala, as his many works reveal. Bobbie, a competent astrologer, had read widely and was particularly knowledgeable on the magical beliefs of the Celts. Both had strong personalities. Bill, born in Aries with a Leo Ascendant – a powerful combination – could not tolerate fools gladly, if at all, while Bobbie, with her natal sun in Cancer, held similar views. So, although they lived under the same roof and were obviously very fond of each other, they made formidable opponents if they happened to disagree on something. I must say that I learned from both of them.

The first time we performed the Rite of Autumn, I officiated as Officer of the West: the principal role for that season. Arnold took the North, and Bill and Bobbie were South and East, respectively. During the meditation period it was customary to sit in one of the four elegant chairs provided, listening to a tape of sea sounds. Very soon I began to feel a surge of energy coming from the West, behind me. It grew stronger and stronger until it enveloped me entirely. I knew it for the great tidal force of Birthing and Becoming, and at that moment *I* was the vehicle for that power. I needed, quite desperately, to give birth to it *through my physical body*; it was taking me over. I realized that I must *control* this manifestation – transmute it into its higher expression of Compassion and allow it to flow to the other Companions in the Circle. I quickly shifted gear, from the sexual to the emotional, and accomplished my intent.

Once, while celebrating Autumn with my friends, I observed a bright flash of light. It occurred so quickly that I wondered whether I had indeed seen it, but after the Rite, Bill said he had also observed it, and we agreed that our eyes had not deceived us. That it manifested from realms other than the material, there was no doubt. I think Bill was pleased with our work, as he announced, 'Do you know, I prefer to perform the Seasonal with you two than with anyone else.'

Bobbie was asked to give a talk on astrology to the local Townswomen's Guild, and, as she hated going to the hairdressers, I offered to perform her tonsorial requirements. Bill came in as I was combing out her hair and exclaimed, 'Good God, Pat, you ought to be a hairdresser. Bobbie's hair looks very good.' Arnold stayed in with Bill while I drove Bobbie to the venue; it was lovely to sit there and be part of the audience for a change. Bobbie gave an excellent and informative lecture, without notes, and supplemented it by drawing the natal charts of famous and infamous people on a blackboard. In the case of criminals and murderers she explained their often difficult planetary configurations, even to the time of their executions.

As I came to know Bobbie better, I discovered that beneath her matter-of-fact and rather brusque exterior there lay a very sensitive soul, whose loyalty to her friends was of the utmost importance.

Bill presented me with copies of several of his works, including *Seasonal Occult Rituals*, together with tapes of his own chants and songs that he incorporated into them. We performed these rituals for twenty-five years. They were most helpful to newcomers and/or those contemplating initiation into the Craft, for the following reasons. Firstly, they enabled people taking part in their initial experience of ritual to become familiar with the orientation of the Circle and the basic symbols of Magic, namely the Sword, Wand, Cup, Shield (Pentacle) and Cord. Secondly, they met other likeminded souls who were already initiates of the Sheffield coven. Therefore, if they were eventually initiated, themselves, they discovered that they were among people *they already knew*. One of the most important aspects of a coven is for the members to be *en rapport* with one another – that is a *must*.

William Gray's book *The Rollright Ritual* (Helios 1975) was the result of his spending the watches of the night at the Rollright Circle in Oxfordshire. His vigils, combined with a heightened psychic perception, brought forth a ritual the very nature and composition of which belongs to an earlier time. Bill often cycled there from Cheltenham, arriving at twilight and just before the rising of a full moon. Here are Bill's own thoughts on the matter:

> I have pointed out that although the Rite 'came through' me, it is not my personal or exclusive property, and the Inners at the Stones seem keen to get those in sympathy with Them to start something regular there. They said they would do it in the end, (but I did not really think they *could* do it, to be quite truthful) . . .
>
> It's the *Pattern* which is of more importance than the words I got through to translate the old intentions behind things. Of course it is like an initiation, for it *is* the Initiation of Life-Death-Life, etc, in the Cosmic Circle we all go through. The idea is to get the Pattern sufficiently deep into the basic consciousness, and the rest should take care of itself like an autopilot.
>
> Oh yes, the Words teach too, because they link on very deep levels of awareness indeed. Whatever 'They' are behind the Rollright Stones, 'They' are certainly a very kindly and beneficent lot, for some reason still very concerned with this land and their living descendants and spiritual dependents in it.

One bright autumn day, we performed the Rollright Ritual at the Rollright Circle, the 'King' stone, and the 'Whispering Knights', with taped music accompanying us as we strolled round the complex. We made the obligatory offering at the 'Whispering Knights' then departed in silence.

During one of our visits, Bill received a message, clairaudiently, and the voice that he heard said he was Gerald Gardner. Towards the end of the message – quite a lengthy one – the voice gave Bill some information that was known only to Gerald and myself and said, 'Pat will know it's me if you tell her that'. As it meant nothing to him, Bill asked if it made any sense to me (which of course, it did). Bill remarked, 'You know, Pat, I never met Gerald Gardner, but from what he has told me just now, he knew a damned sight more about the Mysteries than I previously thought.'

In 1992, Bill and Bobbie passed beyond the Veil – their work well done. They died within three weeks of each other, and are both very sadly missed.

Leslie Roberts was an unbiased investigator of witchcraft and allied subjects, a seasoned traveller who had visited many parts of the world in his search for the magical and mysterious. One evening, he called at Doreen Valiente's home for a chat about the current occult scene. We were sitting round the table when I happened to glance at Leslie, and what I saw I will never forget. Directly behind him a fearful apparition had appeared. It wore a cowl, draped over a skull – a death's head – and had bat-like, leathery wings outspread. I looked quickly at my companions and realized they were unaware of the visitation. When I again looked at Leslie, the vision had vanished.

When Leslie had gone home, I told the others what I had seen. Doreen, naturally shocked at the nasty omen, said that Leslie had but recently come out of hospital. We hoped it had been a figment of my imagination, but it was to prove otherwise. In less than a year, and after being readmitted to hospital, Leslie Roberts passed away.

What I could not understand was why that vision had appeared in such a terrible and frightening form, unlike other, more gentle omens of death I have witnessed. However, in *The Rebirth of Witchcraft* (Robert Hale, 1989) Doreen devotes a chapter to Leslie Roberts, and she mentions a case which Leslie investigated concerning a woman who was haunted by an evil spirit. Although Leslie was familiar with minor hauntings and disturbances, and had experience in this field, it appeared that the darker side of the occult was way out of his league. As a result of the exorcism he performed on the woman to try to rid her of the obsessing entity, Doreen writes, he was never the same man again. Leslie complained of feeling very cold all the time, as if the malignant evil he contacted had somehow attached itself to him. He already had heart trouble, but following this experience his health deteriorated very quickly, almost as though an infestation of dark forces were accelerating his demise. Of course, nothing of this nature could be proved, but it does help to explain why that apparition I saw was such a fearful one.

On one occasion the Sheffield coven worked to obtain a new flat for Doreen Valiente, and in the middle of the working I received the vision of a coffin that refused to be banished. None of the other witches sensed this depressing portent, which was most disturbing to say the least. However, a week later, Doreen rang with the sad news that her husband, Cassie, had passed away. A lecture in Nottingham prevented me from being present at Cassie's funeral, but Arnold and I drove down to Brighton afterwards. We were able to stay with Doreen for a few days, at the time she most needed the company of friends. I was really sorry about Cassie, he was such a straight, no-nonsense type – a really good egg!

Eventually, Doreen obtained a nice modern flat – exactly what she required – and the flurry of moving to new surroundings may have helped, in a very small way, to take her mind off her bereavement.

It was not long before I was once again heading for Brighton. Dorothy, a friend of mine, drove me down, and upon arrival we booked into an hotel. Of course, we called round to see Doreen, and during the conversation I happened to mention that we were staying at 16 Oriental Place. Doreen exclaimed, 'Why, that is the house where Charles Godfrey Leland used to live!' Leland had been a prolific writer on many subjects, not least, witchcraft. His book *Aradia, or the Gospel of the Witches* (1899) resulted from his meeting with Maddalena, a gypsy sorceress in Florence, through whom he was initiated into La Vecchia Religione (the Old Religion) of Italy, which had survived in wild and remote regions of that country (handed down through family ties, much the same as in Britain and elsewhere). Choosing *that* particular hotel was, I thought, a meaningful coincidence.

Members of the Sheffield coven also had their share of psychic occurrences. One concerned Connie, a dear friend and witch, who came from Bolton in Lancashire. She told me of a beautiful experience she had one morning. She was pottering about in her garden tending her flowers, when she caught sight of a little flower growing on its own. As she looked, a tiny light appeared on it and gradually grew brighter and brighter. It was a vivid blue colour, with a faint blue aura, and it slowly expanded until it floated just above the petals. Connie gazed at it, spellbound, for quite some time, then ran indoors to fetch her husband to see it. But when they both returned to the garden the light had gone. It was obviously something especially intended for her: Connie passed over some years ago. She was a beautiful soul, and a true friend in every way.

Another dear friend and initiate of my coven, who passed over in the 1980s, I shall refer to by his magical name, 'Gwion'. He was a professional photographer and a muse-inspired poet of the highest calibre.

Gwion had an impish sense of humour, and when he moved into a cottage in the middle of Wath Woods, near Sheffield, he invited his friends to what he called, a 'Hovel-Warming'. The invitation card also included the following information:

An entertainment programme has been arranged, at no expense, which includes:

Outside Lou – Infamous 100-yard Olympic nocturnal torch-bearer.

Alexis Haunders – Alternating male and female imperson-ations (guess which).

Corré Spondent – with the combined Fleet Street Wail Voice Liars, will sing extracts from *Piddler On The Truth* (guaranteed good for the circulation).

The final item will be a recorded message from the Pope on the subject of 'Rhythm & Booze', or 'How to procreate without really trying'.

During one of our seasons on the Isle of Wight I remember thinking how good it would be if one or two witch friends were to turn up, and we could have a meeting (the festival of Lammas was approaching and had turned my mind in this direction). We were situated at Puckpool, a holiday centre, and one morning as I walked down from Puckpool House (a sixteenth-century manor), I saw a man coming towards me. He waved, and I suddenly recognized Gwion! He and his girl friend were holidaying in the area, so of course we had that meeting!

On Lammas Eve we went to Brading Downs. It was a warm, balmy night and a full moon bathed the land in a silvery radiance. During the rite – and although we were alone on that part of the Downs – everyone felt as if they were being watched. I recalled Gerald telling me of this phenomenon, which he had also experienced – when you thought you were being watched, it was the power gathering and waiting to be told what to do.

Naturally, it occurs in a ritual held outdoors, where the forces of nature are present. What one feels, is the almost tangible, etheric energies pouring from the vegetation in response to the summons and invocations. For this reason, great benefit is accrued from holding meetings in the countryside, especially if there are magical workings to be performed; you do not have to rely solely upon your nerve power, so the exercise is less tiring. In high summer, amid natural surroundings, the invocations at the Four Gates are very powerful, indeed. The etheric emanations are 'on tap', so to speak, and gather almost immediately.

That night, as we danced beneath the Moon, the very grass beneath our feet sparkled with tiny flashes of light – we saw those sparks! After a toast to the Old Ones, we sat quietly, drinking in the magical atmosphere of Lammas Eve on Brading Downs. Before leaving, we poured a libation of wine on to the ground and tossed the remains of our feast into the bushes. As we walked away, it was Gwion who noticed the fox breaking cover from a clump of trees. It stood for a moment, sniffing the air in our direction, then loped off into the undergrowth. Had it been watching us all the time?

The invocations and poetry that Gwion wrote for the Old Religion, have a truly magical quality, and those he gave to me are constantly incorporated into our rituals. I include two of them here, in memory of Gwion.

The Goddess Speaks

I am the reality beyond the myth,
that truth which,
running as sand through your waking thoughts,
forms dream-shapes in sleep,
dissolving too quick to hold.
I am that which you knew a while and lost ere the words rose.
She who scorns your intellect, defies your tongue.

91

I am the silver wisdom within,
burning brighter than the high sun riding the heaven,
leaving you mute,
your broken phrases scorched words,
about your feet.

That which you heard,
ear pressed to the north-wind,
then ever on the tip of your mind.
My beloved -
your brush can give me no form,
your pen no semblance.
All must seek me alone, though, once found . . .

I am She who is with you forever,
whose tears and wrath won you from the darkness,
who calls you child,
who calls you lover -
She who calls you,
She who calls,
SHE.

Samhain

Night of the Dead – black crowded darkness forming the
bridge.
Silent clamour of the returning hoard filling the night but
no space,
and we, hosts in our turn greet in love the Mighty Dead.
All is life, on the Feast of the Dead – on Samhain.

The sword, flashing candle-glow, salutes The Guardians,
forms the Circle, builds again the Castle.
Bridges down, we wait, welcoming, expectant,
feeling again the surge as they cross.
Now with us again – The Clan.
Life force quickens, on the Feast of the Dead – on Samhain.

Now fill the cup to drink in honour of our kin.
Ours by choice and right.
To talk gravely, laugh merrily
as kinsmen will in kinship.

Keeping, with them, the ancient festival.
Out of time, is the time of the Dead – is Samhain.

Borne on no chill wind, this merry crew,
the dead and the Lord of the Dead.
Their rich warmth reaches the soul of us encumbered in
flesh.
Tonight we warm our cold clay at the fire of your caring.
Tonight is the promise renewed, and our spirits drink the
life-force with our beloved dead.
At the hour of the dead – on the Eve of Samhain.

One of Gwion's poems has appeared several times in print, without due acknowledgement to the author. Originally entitled 'The God Speaks', the verse begins: 'I am the God who waits, in the dead of the year, in the dark of life, at the end of the lane . . .'. Yet another gem from Gwion's pen!

Math, another talented individual, also became an initiate of ours. He formed his own group in Scotland, from which has grown many other covens. Personally, I find that male witches are every bit as worthy as females, in respect of their dedication to the Goddess and for their psychic and artistic abilities. Math is no exception. He is a visionary of no mean order, and by profession, a brilliant classical musician.

On one of his visits to Sheffield I took him to see the 'Nine Maidens' stone circle, on Stanton Moor in Derbyshire. (In occultism, nine is considered to be the number of the Moon – and it was recently discovered that the orb's diameter measures 2,160 miles: digits which add up to nine). The legend at the site, reads: 'A Bronze Age stone circle used for religious purposes', an opinion I fully endorse.

A local vicar had reconsecrated these stones, due to what he called 'Black Magic rites and vandalism'. The 'Nine Maidens' had a large blackened area at its centre, where fires had evidently been lit, and the grass was strewn with litter; whoever they were, the culprits cared little for this sacred site, although 'magical' folk may not have been the ones at fault. (Anna Greenwood, a High Priestess of the Goddess and a personal friend of mine, takes her coven to this circle regularly, and, armed with plastic bags, they clean it up and dispose of all the rubbish.) A stone wall originally encircled the site, and a little stile facilitated entry to the circle, but this has now completely vanished, along with another wall which protected the nearby 'King Stone'. Today, the circle has lost its mystery, and the grass no longer grows there.

When I went with Math, I intended to reconsecrate the stones to the Triple Goddess. I thought it was a bit of a cheek for a Christian priest to meddle with a Pagan site! The day was bright and sunny, and Joe Public was out in force on the moor. The chances of performing the consecration unobserved seemed very remote. However, we had been in the vicinity for about half an hour, when quite suddenly, it started to rain. On such a sunny day it seemed incredible, but there it was: an extremely fine, though heavy downpour that resembled a curtain of silvery gauze – quite lovely, really. People scurried like rabbits to get back to their vehicles, a good fifteen minutes' walk away in any direction, and quite soon we had the circle to ourselves.

I reconsecrated the Stones, and I also blessed the 'King Stone', known locally as 'Bill's Stump', a small block about three feet in height that lies north-west of the circle. Towards the end of the ceremony, a surprising thing occurred. Four rams appeared from nowhere, approached the circular wall and then stood, equidistant from each other, facing the Stones. (There were lots of sheep on the open moor nearby; even so, *four rams* standing as if they had been placed there!) As soon as the Rite ended, the rain stopped, the rams departed, and as we strolled back to the car, people were once more walking on the moor. Call it providential if you will, but that is exactly what it was – The Ancient Providence!

The next day, Math took me to see Ruth Wynn-Owen, who lived at Wells-next-the-Sea, in Norfolk. She had had many operations for cancer of the throat, and she was living testimony to the endurance and bravery of the human spirit. I had first met Ruth when Gwion drove me over to the Wentworth Estate, near Barnsley, where she lived. (Her husband, Ian Danby, was related to the Fitzwilliam family who owned the estate, and they lived at Skiers Spring Lodge, a large rambling house set in acres of grounds.) Of Welsh ancestry, she practised the magical tradition of her forebears, handed down through her family and known as the 'Plant Bran'. She was a delightful person and for years had been a professional actress and a teacher of Drama and Voice Production. One of her pupils, the ebullient Brian Blessed (my favourite actor), made it to the top in films and television, and when Brian appeared on *This is your Life* in the role of victim, Ruth was introduced as the person who had coached him for the theatre when he was a young man. In his autobiographical work *The Dynamite Kid* Brian talks about Ruth, and his book carries a lovely picture of her. Strangely, there is also a photograph of the 'Whispering Knights' at the Rollright Stones, captioned, 'friends of my mother's . . .'. They 'talk' to a lot of people!

A tracheotomy meant that Ruth could take only fluids, but she never grumbled. Often she went off to London to help others who had had similar operations and teach them how to articulate their words and improve their speech; she was a petite figure, but what she lacked in size, she certainly made up for in courage. When I visited her in 1991, we sensed that it would be our last meeting in this life. Her condition had seriously deteriorated, so that it was difficult for her to speak at all. She wrote things down, or her friend would know what she wanted to say, and speak for her. Even so, that day Ruth was elated, despite everything. She had received a letter from Dame Peggy Ashcroft, a long-standing friend. Since writing that letter, Dame Peggy had died, so it was very precious to her.

Ruth was full of smiles, and we held hands very tightly – it was enough. I can still see her tiny figure waving from the door of her cottage, as I drove away. Partings of this nature are almost impossible to deal with, so have to be conducted with the utmost grace and control. I'm sure Ruth felt the same.

During a season on the Isle of Wight, I gave my mother a Tarot reading, and I knew that when she returned home, she should not attempt to go upstairs on a bus. I warned her that if she did not follow my advice, there would be an accident. She promised faithfully to do so, but a week or two later a neighbour rang to say that my mother had had an accident on a bus.

Apparently, she had waited for a bus to go shopping, but when it arrived the conductor shouted 'Upstairs only', so she waited for another. It was the same story with the next one. When a third bus came along, she boarded it, but when the doors closed, the call was 'Upstairs only' once again, so upstairs she finally went. When the bus arrived at her destination, though, she stood up and walked to the top of the stairs. At that moment a pedestrian darted into the road, and the driver made an emergency stop. Mother was flung down the stairs and remembered nothing more until she woke up in hospital. She fell on her head and was badly concussed but lucky to be alive. I made the long journey home to be with her, and thankfully she made a full recovery, but for a lady in her seventies, such a fall was definitely not to be recommended.

A strange thing happened when a lovely, intelligent kitten of ours, became very ill and, despite veterinary assistance, died. The following night, when my mother came upstairs to bed, she told me that she had heard our kitten mewing in the dining-room, near the fireplace. I hurried down and stood listening, and, sure enough, there it was: a plaintive little mewing that came out of the silence in the vicinity of the fireplace. I heard nothing more, although I waited for some time.

We loved that little mite, and it seemed so unfair that it had to die so young. Mother was upset, but relieved that I had heard the kitten too, as it confirmed she wasn't going loopy. I prayed to Bast, the ancient Egyptian Cat-Goddess, to protect and guide its little soul. It was so distressing to hear that cry from a creature we had loved so much.

Our next-door neighbours' children brought home a young black cat which they had found wandering. Their parents did not want it, because they had two dogs, so we took possession. He was a real beauty and may have been half-Siamese, as he had the Siamese mask and long, whip-like tail; he also had a small white patch under his throat. We called him Shah.

One day he went missing, and my mother asked a neighbour, two doors away, if she had seen him; the woman said she had seen him earlier in the day, in our garden. Then, for some unknown reason, my mother asked the woman where her daughter-in-law lived, and the neighbour indicated in the general direction of a housing estate and said, 'Oh, over there.' Mother asked for the name of the road and the number of their house. The woman waffled a bit and said they were moving, as the houses were due for demolition. She gave the number 67, but not the actual name of the road.

I wanted to know what on earth was going on. What had these people to do with Shah's disappearance? Mother put on a very mysterious expression and said, 'There is a terrace of old houses at the bottom of that estate, and if you go to number 76, you will find Shah.' I stared at her, 'But how do you know that?' My parent gave me an old-fashioned look and replied, 'I just feel it in my bones. If she knows he *is* there, she will have reversed the number of their house.'

That same evening, accompanied by my friend, Beryl, I walked down to the far end of the housing estate. It was a damp, foggy night with a drizzle of fine rain, and when we came to the dismal terrace of houses, we stood and contemplated our next move. As we crossed the road, I thought of that 'new' number, '76', but many of the houses had lost their numbers, and in any case their 'front' doors were in passages at the side of the dwellings. We came to the first passage, and Beryl said, 'Let's go down this one.' It led to the rear of two houses, one on either side. The light from a window of the house on the left, filled the yard, but everything was very quiet.

Then, my friend hissed, 'He's here!', and, sure enough, Shah came running to us. I grabbed him and we ran back to the road. 'Wait a minute,' I gasped. 'We'd better make quite sure it *is* Shah and not another black cat.' So we had a proper look at him under the yellow gleam of a street light. Yes, there was the white patch under his throat that looked like a bow-tie. Beryl zipped him safely inside her jacket, while I, very daring, went back to the passage and shone my torch on the door of the house. It was number 76! We darted away into the fog feeling like a pair of thieves – which was odd considering the circumstances.

Thinking back, we realized that Shah had been left outside near a busy road, and Beryl said that he seemed to enter the yard with us. So, we presumed that he must have been on the handkerchief-sized patch of grass at the front of the house, and we had not seen him because the night was so foggy. (Lucky for us, he *was* outside!) When we got home we rang the bell and put on doleful expressions when my mother came to the door. Then Beryl opened her jacket, and Shah's head popped out. Mother threw up her hands, her face beaming with happiness: 'Oh, you've found him. Bless you!'

Shah was made much of in the weeks that followed (and indeed for the rest of his long life). We decided to keep him indoors until he grew a bit more though as we did not relish 'losing' him again.

Arnold wanted to know what I would say if I bumped into our neighbour. 'Oh, I'll think of something,' I grinned. When I did happen upon her, she enquired if I had got my cat back, or something to that effect. 'Oh yes, we did,' I replied, 'and my friend says if she sees him round there in the future, she will bring him back again,' which was perfectly true. And that was the end of that, thanks entirely to my mother's sixth sense!

Requests to open fetes or judge competitions became commonplace beginning with the Stray Cat's Sanctuary cat show in Bradford. A particularly fateful dance was held one 'Friday the 13th' at which I judged the fancy-dress competition, on the theme of Witches & Magicians. At this event I met a girl who was to become a close friend. Anne was a fraternal twin, born under the sign of Libra, and, as is usual with fraternal twins, one of them is orthodox in beliefs and attitudes, while the other is unconventional and clever. Like Arnold, (another Libran), Anne was the 'different' twin. She played the accordion and piano, and we enjoyed musical evenings with both our families. Her parents, Bill and Mary, were avid card players, which suited me down to the ground, as I adore card-games.

When I first met Anne, her work consisted of ferrying large American cars from London to Sheffield, and when she stopped at a service station, lorry drivers, with sarcastic grins, would enquire, 'Did Daddy buy it for you?' Anne had a great sense of humour and was never at a loss when a sharp riposte was required. 'No,' she would reply. 'I'm driving this car because the Rolls is in for a service today.' And off she would go, leaving her tormentors with the grins stuck uncomfortably to their faces.

Anne was interested in psychic matters and also in reincarnation, although she had never studied occultism *per se.* When she expressed a desire to discover something of her previous lives, I took her through the basic instructions on scrying for several months. When the time seemed right, I decided to perform a mirror working with her. This is much the same as scrying into a crystal ball, or any other reflective surface. It quietens and subdues the conscious mind, and allows the subconscious to reveal something of what it knows of the soul's previous lives – and it is said to know a great deal. If this is so, there must be some link between the subconscious mind and the soul because, apart from the Astral Body, the soul is the only part of us that survives physical death. Taina Ketala, in her book, *The New Astrology*, says, 'All memories, whether stemming from a past life or the present life, are not stored in the brain but in the soul.'

The method of scrying is as old as the hills, and, whether the seer is aware of it or not, activates the pineal gland, known in ancient times as the Third Eye. This gland, situated centrally in the brain, beams out between the eyes, in the centre of the forehead. The Ancient Egyptians acknowledged it by painting a third eye in this position on their statuary, and it was recognized in most parts of the ancient world. Through the art of scrying, a person can become aware of the reasons which necessitated their present incarnation. I was no exception.

In a darkened room with a strategically placed lighted candle, I performed a preliminary invocation, then Anne and I sat quietly, gazing into the mirror so that both our reflections were visible in it. After a time, I began to see actual scenes of a particular country, manifesting somewhere between the mirror and where I was sitting, as though I was viewing a film. I sensed a hot country and saw myself wearing a long, white dress, while another younger person (Anne?), wore a short tunic with what looked like violets in her hair. I knew without any doubt, that I had a position of authority there, and as the visions continued they brought an inner knowledge of being angry or upset with this person, because of their behaviour at the time.

Another scene informed me of the punishment I had meted out to my companion, through certain men who were guards or soldiers, and I was not sure whether the 'culprit' survived this punishment, or not. (Neither was I certain as to the gender of the person involved, but that is of little consequence.) The visions evoked strong emotions from the deep wells of my spirit, and the tears coursed down my face as I watched and realized, very clearly, what those scenes were telling me. Certainly, the innermost depths of my being were plumbed and called forth to merge with them. There were no sounds – no sobs – my soul alone 'wept'.

When the visions ceased and the speculum reverted to being just a mirror, we continued to sit there silently, and I wondered what Anne had seen – if anything. Eventually, I asked her, and she began to talk. Like me, she had observed the sunlit vistas of a hot clime, and had seen herself dressed in a short tunic with flowers in her hair. Anne had also recognized me as her companion, and said we had been squabbling about something on a sun-baked path. She had seen nothing more – but even this much was astonishing for someone who was attempting to scry for the first time.

The more harrowing details, such as the punishment, had been concealed from her, which in a curious way enhanced the veracity of the visions. After all, they were associated with my own Karma, and thus were personal to me. Therefore, I did not enlighten her on those details. I thought, 'So – that is why we have met again in this life, under the same Sun sign: to settle a Karmic debt,' and I trembled, inwardly, for what was to come.

It is stressed in the Mysteries that, in order to redress negative Karma involving another soul, one of them can be drawn into the embryo of a fraternal twin, in order to be reborn in the same time continuum as the other soul. This may be an automatic reaction – a compulsory Karmic event. Nevertheless, I understood why I had such a depth of feeling for Anne. We might have been 'an item' centuries ago, or even a married couple! (A dim echo of that incarnation occurred many years later, while I was walking in the heat of a summer's day, complete with a heavy shopping-bag. As I toiled along, the road and the buildings vanished, and I was treading a dusty path in a long white robe, with sandals on my feet. A moment out of time!)

That the visions were a warning of future trials between Anne and myself I had no doubt, and it was not long before they began. A flurry of small arguments erupted, which often grew out of proportion, although we patched them up and became friends, again. This pattern was repeated times without number, but Anne was a restless soul, forever seeking new people and new situations. She moved away from her parents' home and also joined an amateur singing group, regaling me with stories of her new friendships which hurt me much more than they should have done.

Arnold was a tower of strength through it all, as was my mother, who liked Anne and her family very much, but (unlike Arnold, in whom I had confided) my mother did not understand why we quarrelled. She wondered what all the pother was about, and said as much.

I prayed to the Goddess, constantly, asking for strength of spirit, and guidance. I wanted Anne to remain my friend – my special friend – and for us to continue our happy times together, but in my heart I knew it was not to be. And as I strove to hold on to her, she became more and more distant.

One of the most important links between us was laughter, believe it or not. Anne was a great mimic with a neat turn of phrase, and it reminded me of those times in the theatre, when there was always something to giggle about.

Once, while communing with the Goddess, a flood of words came into my head, and I wrote them down immediately. It was a story, and it informed me that, no matter what happened to our friendship, I must keep loving Anne, and that love was the only way out of the torment.

In essence, I am a simple, uncomplicated soul, who trusts the Ways of the Gods, implicitly. But there is another side to my nature, a commanding, leadership influence – at times even imperious – that I know reverts to a former lifestyle, and is echoed in my Leo Ascendant. Hardly ever allowed to surface, it has been subjugated and transformed into the ghost of its former self, and now manifests as generousness.

Arnold was given instructions from the Goddess, and this

wisdom was of tremendous help in the situation. And so the day came when we had our final disagreement. I rushed upstairs, not knowing what I was doing, and passed out on the bedroom carpet. Arnold and Mum came quickly, picked me up and carried me to bed, where I eventually regained my senses.

I felt so awful for putting them through such pain, and I loved them all the more for the trouble I was causing them. How could I have been so selfish? Anne and I were good friends for a time, and if she (as male or female) was once a lover of mine in a previous life, whom I had wronged for some reason, the Karmic balance must now surely be restored. And, indeed it had! Arnold and I still visited Anne's parents, or they came to us, and I saw Anne, too, from time to time, but those deep feelings for her had gone, or became sublimated, and that must have been the best thing for all concerned.

Initiation evokes both positive and negative Karma. Putting your feet once more upon The Path is not a step to be taken lightly. However, if you put your trust in the Goddess and Her Consort, always (but always!) the Divine Pair will grasp your hands and help you through any adversity. An apt simile from Gray's *Seasonal Occult Rituals* comes to mind: 'Who enters life is past recall, for none may rise, but they that fall – above is reached, below.'

Through adherence to the Old Religion, my life has grown richer in many ways. Occultists and witches who bear the name 'friend' have added to my knowledge in the discipline of Magic, each soul contributing a unique insight into a particular aspect. The way in which we interpret things is infinitely varied, but there is a useful analogy in the colours of the rainbow, and the manner in which they blend to project a harmonious and beautiful design.

6 Dark Clouds and Silver Linings

Saturn in the Fourth House of my natal chart, indicated that one area of life-learning would take place in the environs of the home. Saturn is the Teacher of the Zodiac, and by its placement also reveals where negative Karma will be encountered. However, on the positive side, Saturn is situated in Sagittarius and is at ease here, the planet bestowing a love of learning and a sense of honour. Numerology gives to Saturn the number seven, a number that is also echoed in my name and date of birth. Seven has long been considered as a number of initiation and mystery. Other than the above, there are no adverse or difficult Karmic aspects in the chart as the Twelfth House is free from affliction. And what is known as the 'Sign of Protection' (the symbol of Arachne, the Spider Goddess) stands in the House of Fate.

With the dawning of the seventies, it was not too difficult to anticipate that the most arduous period of my life was at hand. Tests and trials of which I had never dreamed, would call for the utmost resilience and courage.

The relationship with Anne, at the very beginning of that decade, gave more than an inkling of what was in store, though it is often only through hindsight that one can see the pattern that has emerged. I called that decade my *bête noire*, although I realized from the information given in my natal chart that it was something I needed to go through in this present life. Even so, not everything was gloom and doom. There were bright flashes of happiness at the start of the decade and also near its end.

103

In March 1970 I achieved one of my objectives. This was to have an article accepted by *Prediction*, a long-established monthly magazine featuring astrology and the occult. Entitled 'The Truth about Britannia', it was to be the first of many articles of mine to appear in *Prediction* and other periodicals of the time. Evidently, my work, and that of other writers, satisfied the needs of readers whose interest in our pagan past had been newly awakened.

Another dream was fulfilled, with the purchase of a three-hundred-year-old cottage in Whitby. Situated on East Cliff in the Old Town, it is a perfect hideaway where I can escape from the stresses of life, and dwell awhile in seclusion, with only the lapping of the incoming tides and the cries of sea-gulls, for company.

Eight steps lead down to the beach, and nearby stands the old Tate Hill Pier where, according to Bram Stoker's famous novel, Dracula came ashore from the ship which had brought him from his homeland in Transylvania. On winter nights, the wind rushes, moaning, through the ancient alleyways, and at high-tide the waves crash against the quayside, then run up the steps, as if seeking out an unwary traveller.

Whitby is known as 'The Haven under the Hill' and still keeps its unique atmosphere and its ancient fishermen's cottages built close to the water. On nights when a sea mist rolls in and wraps the town in a shroud of grey vapour, the foghorn booms dismally at regular intervals, reminding its inhabitants in their cosy, brightly-lit homes of the menfolk out at sea. Those sturdy, stone-built cottages have been the homes of fishermen, their wives and families for a very long time, and many still live there. Others are now the homes of artists and writers, or people who come to this place and find they are unable to leave it. Once seen, Whitby draws you back, and you are never again quite free from it – nor wish to be.

Arnold and I spent many weekends at Whitby, and one visit happened to coincide with the Summer Solstice. We thought it would be a good idea to watch the midsummer sunrise from the top of the cliffs, so we rose very early and climbed the famed 199 steps – the Church Stairs – that lead to St Mary's church and thence to the headland.

It was eerie in that half-light before the dawn. We passed

the graveyard, where tombstones lean in the sloping ground that leads to the edge of the cliffs, as if awaiting their turn to plummet into the waves. (Among the graves is a bench called 'Lucy's seat', which dates from the time when *Dracula* was first filmed there.) On the headland a strong, cold wind was blowing off the sea and carrying frozen particles of ice from the far north. It beat against our faces as we gazed hopefully at the lightening grey clouds above an equally grey sea. Could this really be the Summer Solstice? There was something in the air that morning – a foreboding, which created apprehension at Nature's off-putting disposition and a certain feeling of unease.

We spoke little, shrugging deeper into our clothing as we stood there, aimlessly. Arnold said, 'Too much cloud. The sun must have risen by now. Let's go.' I thought of 'Moon-tide' (the name I gave to our cottage), and breakfast with steaming mugs of coffee, and quickly agreed.

As we neared the coastguard station I noticed the solitary figure of a policeman standing there. My eyes were watering in the cold air, and I rubbed them to make sure I was not mistaken. What on earth was the Law doing out here on the cliffs so early?

It soon became obvious that he was waiting for us. We exchanged a polite 'Good morning', and the officer asked us what we were doing on the cliff-top at that hour of the day. Apparently the coastguard had telephoned the police to say there were two people wandering about on the headland; he thought they were up to no good and might be signalling to someone out at sea, or helping illegal immigrants into the country. I could not believe what I was hearing, and started to giggle, but Arnold remarked, calmly, 'Well, it *is* the longest day, isn't it?' Then he explained our reasons for being there at that time. The light dawned, and the officer grinned, 'Oh, I see, the Summer Solstice, eh?' We grinned back, nodding. 'Not much chance of seeing it today, and it's well past sunrise, now,' he commented, consulting his watch. I told him that we had a cottage nearby and that we were now returning to it to get warm. 'Yes,' he smiled. 'Sorry for the mix-up, but you can't be too careful these days.' We agreed you could not, and he waved us cheerily on our way.

Walking down the steps, I said, 'Fancy that! The coast-guard thinking we were doing something illegal, and informing the police, too!' Arnold shrugged, 'Well, I suppose he was only doing his duty and reporting anything unusual.' Nonetheless, quite apart from that singular incident, I will never forget the chill foreboding that bitter dawn evoked in me, and the years that followed bore out those fears.

Arnold's illness revealed itself in the summer of 1973, and he passed away on Beltane, 1 May 1974. I will not dwell upon the terrible strain of that unhappy time, but I must relate a curious incident concerning it.

Several years earlier we had been driving home from Coventry one night in a very thick pea-souper. We passed slowly through Nuneaton, and the fog got worse than ever. It was almost impossible to drive, so we pulled on to the fore-court of a garage which had long since closed for the night. Some ten minutes later, headlights loomed out of the fog, and another vehicle stopped on the forecourt; the driver got out and came over to us. (It was long before the days of the muggings and other offences prevalent today; nevertheless, we wondered about the dark figure approaching our car that fog-bound night.) A male voice hailed us, commented on the foul weather and enquired if we had far to go. Arnold said that we were a considerable distance from home – too far to attempt the journey for the time being. The stranger suggested that we stay with him for the night, as he lived only a mile away. We were unsure of the situation, but eventually agreed to follow the lights of his car, if he led the way.

At a snail's pace we tailed his vehicle until it turned left on to a narrow lane which ran between high hedges. Soon his right indicator winked, and he drove through tall gateposts surmounted by stone effigies of griffin-like creatures. Where on earth was he leading us? It must be some country estate, and of a considerable size. The drive wound between trees and shrubbery until we stopped in front of what looked like a baronial hall. We heard an owl, hooting in the woods, and Arnold whispered, 'It must be Dracula's Castle!' I didn't answer, because his comment did nothing to allay my fears, or the coldness of my bones. I was also dog-tired now, after driving so slowly and straining to see the road ahead for hours on end; my watch showed that it was almost 2 a.m.

The fog swirled round us as we stepped from the car. Our host beckoned us to follow him up broad steps leading to the main entrance. I thought it looked strange, because there was not a glimmer of light to be seen anywhere; the large windows merely stared blankly into the fog. I wished we had remained at the garage, but Arnold was already guiding me up the steps.

The stranger opened the massive door and we followed him inside – still no lights! He produced a torch, whose light revealed the blackened, charred interior of a large entrance hall. The place was a ruin! The torch picked out a wide staircase running up into the darkness; chandeliers, dripping cobwebs, hung dismally from the ceiling, and fallen plaster covered the floor. This house had been burned at some time.

'But . . .' I cried, 'what? . . .' and I took an involuntary step back to the door, pulling at Arnold's sleeve. 'Over here!' called our guide and started to climb a small staircase, hugging the wall to the right of the door, which looked fairly safe. We climbed up behind him as he unlocked another door at the top. 'This is it,' I thought. 'If we go through that door, we may never be seen again.'

Amazingly, there was bright light coming from beyond the door, and a woman was standing in it. Our rescuer explained how he had found us and brought us back with him for a few hours until daylight came, and we entered a large, cheerful room which was difficult to associate with what lay behind us. Soon we were ensconced in comfy armchairs, drinking piping hot coffee and eating buttered scones. Oh, the normality of it!

Our benefactor – whose name, I believe, was Roy – told us that this was Caldecote Hall, which had originally belonged to the Townsend family. Eventually the property was sold and became a hospital for the mentally ill, until one of the patients set fire to it. Some of the rooms that were untouched by the fire were leased as flats, and, as Roy's work was nearby, he and his wife were living there for the time being.

For what was left of the night we dozed to the crackle of a wood fire, and I wished that I lived there, in that lovely peaceful atmosphere. In the early morning light, I looked out of a window; the fog was clearing, and through the tangle of overgrown trees a steel-grey glimmer revealed a lake. Soon, we were heading for Sheffield – and in due course we sent our hosts a special gift for their kindness.

When Arnold became very ill, it was decided that he should have an exploratory operation, so he was admitted to the City General Hospital in Sheffield, where I visited him twice a day. On one visit he remarked, 'I had quite a surprise, this morning.' He beckoned to a male nurse in a white coat further down the ward. When he approached I suddenly recognized Roy, our friendly, midnight guide from Caldecote Hall.

As I shook his hand a shiver unaccountably slid down my spine as I thought of the circumstances in which we had first met. Gracious Mother! That a man should emerge from nowhere, on a foggy night, to be encountered again during my husband's desperate illness – and for this same person to be actually nursing Arnold! Could Roy have been someone from one of Arnold's previous lives – one in which Arnold had helped *him* in some way? It was uncanny. Life became a miasmic blur for many months, but I recall Roy ringing me after Arnold's passing and expressing his condolences.

Three days before Arnold's death he experienced the 'rise of the life-force' which sometimes occurs before the death of the body. He looked and felt well enough to write to some of his friends. Then, on the day he was brought home, the ambulance was late bringing him. The anxiety of waiting brought on some kind of heart attack, but Arnold held on until he was wheeled into the house. I put my arm around him, and with great difficulty he raised his head to look at me, whispered, 'Hello, my darling' and then died.

Mysterious occurrences were to follow my husband's passing, and it was strange how the dates of particular events reduced to the number 9, including the date of his death – 1 May 1974 ($1+5+1+9+7+4=27=9$). The 1st and 8th, too, (the latter the day of Arnold's funeral). It was reminiscent of Gerald's fateful '9'.

When a loved one passes on, it is amazing how you are able to cope and see that everything is performed for the beloved, to the best of your ability. Fellow witches, my mother and other friends rallied round – they were absolute bricks. Arnold had expressed a wish to have a Scottish piper at his last rites. He was entitled to this tribute – his mother had been a Scot, born on the Isle of Mull – so I rang the local Caledonian Society and secured the services of a piper (apparently such requests were commonplace for them). Math, the Scottish High Priest, came down to officiate for the 'Passing Rite', and I thanked him for making the long journey from Scotland. Around two hundred mourners attended, including witches, professional artistes and stage magicians who had known and respected Arnold. I suppose that for many present that day, it was the first time they had witnessed a pagan Passing Rite.

The weather was sunny and warm, and the ceremony was held at the grave-side, although the doors of the Christian chapel were open for us. Math spoke well and, with his dark hair and handsome features, looked every inch a High Priest, his tall, commanding figure clothed in a purple robe.

When he had finished speaking, the piper stepped forward; bowed to me, as the widow of a man who had had Scottish blood in his veins, and played *The Flowers of the Forest* and *The Piper's Lament*. He played them beautifully, too, as I recall. The bagpipes always thrill me, for they speak of ancient things, but that day they skirled for Arnold Crowther, who had loved Scotland.

The music ended abruptly, as bagpipe music usually does, but there followed a distinct sound – that of a brook, or mountain rill, chuckling and murmuring, as over stones in its bed.

Several friends accompanied us back to the house, one of whom, Joyce Woodhouse, asked me 'Did you hear the sound of running water after the pipes had finished?' I assured her that I had indeed heard something like that, and Ethel, a sister witch, commented that she too had heard it and had actually looked behind her, thinking that someone was pouring water into a vessel, nearby.

I had invited the piper to take some refreshments with us, and asked him about it. Was it possible for the sound to have come from the pipes themselves? He shook his head and declared that once the music had finished, there was no further sound from the pipes; he was quite adamant about it, saying, 'Madam, *you* should know, having worked in Scotland for so many years.' (I hastened to reassure him that I was not criticizing his musical dexterity, and complimented him on his playing.) The piper then caught sight of a framed picture of Arnold, and declared, 'But I know this laddie. I have often spoken to him in the course of my work in the city. Just in passing, ye ken.' Another strange twist of fate, for Arnold to have passed the time of day with a stranger who would eventually play at his funeral!

The sound of that running water remained a mystery for some time, until the day I obtained a copy of *Through the Gates of Death*, by Dion Fortune (Aquarian Press, 1957). As I held this book, it fell open at a particular page, where I read the following passage:

> When spiritual love is coming to us from the Inner Planes we have only to still the outer senses for a moment to hear it *purling like a brook*, a steady flow, coming to us all the time from the eternal and steadfast soul that has gone ahead to the Next Country [my emphasis].

Fortune calls it the 'Brook of Love', or the 'Communion of Love', and tells us that no psychic powers are needed for it to reach the mundane consciousness. She advises us to send back our own personal flow of love to our loved one(s) on the Inner Planes.

This, then, was an explanation of the phenomenon we had experienced at the grave-side. Fortune had known of it, and no doubt it was recognized and understood by occultists before *her*, but it was all the more precious to me because I was not familiar with it. When I thought about it, this 'Brook of Love' seemed to have issued from the *inner* ear (the sound of water from the Astral Plane?), manifesting in exactly the same manner as clairaudience.

Jim Couttie, another Scottish witch, came to Arnold's funeral, and stayed the night with us. The next morning he came downstairs looking quite pale. 'Whatever's the matter, Jim?' I asked, and gave him a hot cup of tea laced with whisky (he looked as though he needed it). Jim said he had woken up in the middle of the night to find a hand on his pillow – just a hand! Asked, how he could see it in the dark, he replied,

'Because it was glowing with light.' He said he dived under the bedclothes. Later, though, he realized that it might have been connected with Arnold – perhaps it was Arnold's way of thanking him for coming from Scotland.

I took my mother to Whitby a few months later, but it was some time before I heard what had occurred during our absence. A lady from the neighbourhood stopped me in the street and said, 'Wasn't it strange about Arnold?' When I enquired what she meant, she went on, 'Well, I said it wouldn't be *him*. It was probably his twin brother.' On pressing her for an explanation, I was informed that our next-door neighbour, June, had told people she had seen Arnold. I said that Arnold and his brother Norman had been *fraternal* twins, not identical twins, and so were entirely dissimilar in both appearance and character. I also mentioned how Norman had collapsed and died in Wimbledon, at the time of Arnold's funeral.

I left the lady with a bewildered expression on her face and rushed round to see June. She explained, 'Oh, it was last July, when you and your mother went away. You remember that you had some trouble locking the back door, and I promised to keep an eye on the house?' I nodded, 'And? . . .'. June then told me how one morning she accompanied her children to school as usual, and looked over the dividing wall to see if the back of our house was in order. She thought she heard the back gate open, but everything was quiet. When she returned, she again looked over the wall, and saw a man standing at our back door, looking through the dining-room window. 'I'm sorry,' she said, 'Mrs Crowther and her mother have gone away, and they are not due back for another week or so.' The man turned his head and smiled at her. 'Oh God! Arnold!' cried June and rushed indoors. She told her husband, and he ran to the wall, but there was no one there.

'But, what did he look like?' I cried. 'Oh, just as Arnold always looked,' she replied. 'He looked just the same. He was wearing a dark suit, with his hair sleeked back – Oh yes, it was definitely Arnold all right.'

The experience had obviously made a deep impression upon June, and she was adamant about whom she had seen. So, there it was. The mere fact that the vision had turned and smiled at her revealed the *presence of consciousness*. It was an actual manifestation, not an imprint on the aether – a kind of photographic image – which some apparitions can be. Neither was the appearance of 'clothing', unusual, for the Astral Body often appears as the soul *visualizes* itself.

The amorphic vapour of the Astral Body is moulded by the emotions of the soul that inhabits it. But, once that soul has grown beyond the need of such a body, the material from which it was made disintegrates and returns to the fluidic mass of which the Astral Plane is composed – in exactly the same manner as water poured into a lake from a container. While *in* the container, the water is the same *shape* as the container, until it is poured away.

Of course, I was thrilled to hear of Arnold's 'visit', and although I never saw him in a vision of this kind, he often gave me messages, mostly passed from mind to mind or through clairaudience. Once he came through and said, 'Give my regards to the "Duchess of Duke Street".' He used to tease my mother by giving her this title (she had once lived in Duke Street), and I thought it was something Arnold had made up until a television serial entitled *The Duchess of Duke Street* appeared. It portrayed the life of one Rosa Lewis, a fashionable cook, born in 1867. Her first employer was Lady Randolph Churchill and during her life Rosa Lewis, like my mother, became a hotel-owner. So, my apologies to Arnold!

I remembered Arnold's art of rope-spinning, but could not find the rope anywhere, so I thought back to the last time he had used it, which was a Punch and Judy show. Locating the case of glove puppets, I found the rope tucked away at the bottom (then, clutching 'Punch' in my arms, I sat down and cried my eyes out). I practised rope-spinning in the garden. I was determined to become proficient, so that I could include it in my act. The children had always enjoyed trying to spin the rope in the past, and many of them were good at it, too.

While engaged in this trial-and-error process, I heard a soft chirruping behind me, and there, sitting on the window-sill, was a baby blue tit. It was so tiny with its vivid blue and yellow feathers, and bright little eyes – quite exquisite! When they leave the nest, baby blue tits take to the air; they don't have to learn to fly. Arnold once said that when he met me he knew he had found Maeterlinck's 'Blue Bird of Happiness', and here was this tiny bird – this blue bird!

BBC Radio Bristol expressed an interest in serializing Arnold's autobiographical story, *Hand in Glove*. Julia Donaldson was enthusiastic about the idea of adapting it for radio. However, a sudden commitment sent her to Brighton, so Andrew Smith took over her position as Short Story Editor and recorded *Hand in Glove* in ten episodes, with Douglas Leach as the reader. It was broadcast every Friday, from 18(!) October, to 20 November 1974, and the similarity between the actor's voice and Arnold's was quite unreal; it could almost have been Arnold speaking: Douglas made the story come to life in a very special way, and Andrew Smith commented that Arnold's fascinating career made for compelling listening.

Hand in Glove was subsequently broadcast by Radio Sheffield, Radio Medway, Radio Chatham (Arnold's birthplace) and Radio Leeds. Mother and I were thrilled and would sit listening to it – me, with the tears streaming down my face.

Before it went on air in Sheffield, I was interviewed about Arnold's life and career in front of a studio audience, and I included an amusing incident concerning one of his engagements. A particular booking took him to a large country house where the butler showed him into the room reserved for the show. Arnold noticed that the house was very quiet; there were no sounds of happy children's voices to be heard, nor any signs of a party in progress. Presently, a rather dignified old lady came in, introduced herself and shook his hand. Arnold enquired, 'Where are the children?' The lady replied, 'Oh, there are no children here. I booked your entertainment for my parrot. He always enjoys a show at Christmas.' Arnold thought she must be a bit batty, but he kept a straight face, and, sure enough, the parrot was brought into the room by the butler. Arnold performed his show for the bird and its mistress. He was receiving a handsome fee for his services, and he always believed that he who pays the piper calls the tune. It was the quietest show he had ever done, and the only one in which he actually got the bird!

My mother passed away eighteen months after my

husband. She broke her thigh in an accident which, with the subsequent complications, proved fatal. The night before the accident occurred, I received a strange omen. I was awakened by an owl which hooted three times; it sounded so close that the bird must have been sitting on the sill of the open window. 'Oh no,' I thought, 'this means trouble.' (It was not the owl itself bringing ill-luck, though; the bird was merely warning me of its imminent arrival.)

Soon after my mother's passing, her friend Ida (who is now in her ninety-seventh year) rang to say she had something to tell me, and would I call round. I was in a terrible state; I could not believe I was now alone in the house, bereft of my nearest and dearest – except, that is, for my lovely cats, who were a blessing at this time.

Ida told me she had been standing at the window, looking into her garden and thinking of my mother. She said that she had been there for some time, when something moved across her vision. She described it as a dark, human shape, outlined with a bright band of light. As it glided past she thought, 'Oh, it's Clare, and she's going.' The vision, darkly-clad and appearing three days after death, would suggest that my mother's spirit had newly awakened from the customary three days' sleep and was clothed in its Astral Body. (Incidentally, my mother had requested the 'Passing Rite' at her funeral and had asked Gwion to perform it. This was done.)

Some months later, I was in bed one night trying to read a book before switching off the light, but I felt very miserable and could not settle to read. As I lay there gazing into space, I found myself looking at a little pair of feet. (A pair of feet, hanging in the air? – I must be going loopy! Next stop, the nut-house!) Looking upwards, I saw a figure clothed in white light. The face of the vision was young and lovely, and the lady held out her arms to me. Strangely, I was not awed by the apparition, and merely thought, 'I wonder who *that* is,' as it slowly disappeared.

My bedside light was still switched on, and I lay thinking of what I had seen. It *could* have been my mother, as it slightly resembled photographs of her taken in her twenties, although the features of the vision were ethereal and quite transformed – as one would expect. If it was, the vision, composed of light, would suggest that my mother's spirit had gained a Plane more refined than the Astral.

The following night I was reading in bed when I seemed to drift off. Immediately, I heard my mother's voice, saying, 'Violetta – Violetta – Violetta.' The words were pronounced very slowly, with each vowel drawn out, and the voice came out of my left ear. It shot me awake. However, it was not until much later that I recalled a conversation I had had with my mother some time before she died. I said to her, 'When one of us shuffles off this mortal coil, let us have a special word to pass between us, so that the one who is left behind will know there has been a definite contact.' Mother laughed, 'Yes, but I hope I go before you do.' I had racked brains trying to think of a suitable word, then Mother said, 'Why not have "Violetta"? You did so well with "Hear my song, Violetta" in the theatres.' So that was the word we chose, and that was the word she passed to me from beyond the Veil. It was enough – I felt at peace.

One day I was looking through a drawer in the sideboard, when two unframed pictures propped upon it, did a little dance! They jiggled about, then behaved like normal pictures and stood still. They just happened to be of the God and the Goddess!

My aunt Elsie died the day before my mother, so there were two funerals in the family on consecutive days. Some months later, I took a friend for a run in the car; Agnes was feeling depressed, so I thought a drive might cheer her up. On an impulse, I decided to call on my cousin Sheila (Elsie's daughter). We have always been very close.

Sheila and her husband, Dennis, have a gracious house, but when we arrived, the only person at home was Uncle Sam, Sheila's father. As I returned to the car, I glanced back at the house, where a curtain moved at an upstairs window and a woman's face peered out. I remarked to Agnes, 'That's funny. There is someone upstairs, and Uncle said he was on his own for a while. It must be the cleaner.' Later, talking to Sheila, she was quite adamant that she had left her father on his own that afternoon. We stared at each other. Had I seen a ghost? And if so, whose ghost was it?

When I thought about it, the face of the woman *had* looked like a younger version of Auntie Elsie, so we agreed that it must have been Sheila's late mother. My cousin said that the bedroom with the window in question, had been her younger daughter Diana's before she married, and Elsie, being particularly fond of Diana, had often sat there and talked with her.

There was a further mystical occurrence around that time. One night some words came into my head, so I wrote them down. At first, I thought it was nonsense, until I recognized one of the words: Mort. I also felt impelled to draw a design at the time. I was all agog to know what, if anything, the words meant.

The next day I passed a second-hand bookshop which had a table of books outside; two of them were Latin primers, which I purchased for a few shillings. I located all the words of the 'message', and their English translations, but they did not make much sense to me at the time. They were as follows: *Telum omnis pessime fiat ille mort sequor perdua.* *Telum* = weapon/missile/dart; *omnis* = all/everything/the Universe; *pessime* = badly; *fiat* = declare/proclamation; *ille* = those/that; *mort* = death; *sequor* = follow/come after; *perdua* = endure/hold out/go with. I could only assume that they came from a discarnate spirit conversant with Latin!

I asked around, and one witch-friend, Liz, said she had taken the language at school, so I showed the message to her. She came up with two possible meanings: 'I follow that dart of death – everything endures!' or 'Proclamation: Everything comes after that ill dart of death – endure!' Perhaps a reader can offer a more precise interpretation? On the whole, though, the words appeared to be reassuring.

The design I had drawn was also intriguing, being a stylized drawing of a flower resembling a tulip, and it clearly represented the Four Elements. The petals of the flower personified a crown, or consummation of the whole, and if the symbol was reversed it became a dart. Or was that perhaps the correct way to view it?

A special person helped me through these times of sorrow, whom I will always regard as being 'Goddess sent'. This was a gentleman by the name of Nicholas Barcynski, who sometimes used the name Sandys. He came to live in Sheffield in 1973. Although Nicholas was a man in his sixties, he had retained a certain *joie de vivre* and had many interests, including magic and the worship of the Old Gods, to whom he was devoted.

Nicholas was a gentleman in every sense of the word; he had impeccable manners, and an air of good breeding. Of Polish extraction, he was the son of Countess Barcynska, an author of novels such as *The Honey Pot*. Her second marriage was to a Welshman – the writer Caradoc Evans, whose critical work, *My People*, caused a furore in Wales when it was first published. (In recent times, BBC Radio Cardiff discussed it in a programme which featured Nicholas, Caradoc's stepson.)

Nicholas first came to see us at the beginning of Arnold's illness, and thereafter was a tower of strength to us all. He would sit and talk to Arnold when he was confined to bed, and keep his mind occupied with a variety of topics. In the months following my bereavements, Nicholas was a great comfort, and in the evenings, while partaking of a drop of the hard stuff, he would listen sympathetically while I went over and over the details of those sad times. He understood very well, having lost his own mother not long before.

Nicholas left the district in 1980, but wherever he happened to be, he always wrote and sent his love to 'Dear Shah', my beloved cat. Some years later, he rang and talked of returning to Sheffield, then quite suddenly, around 1986, his communications ceased. I contacted his last known address, a hotel in Westcliff-on-Sea, but he had left there, and, try as I might, I never did find out what became of him.

It was just not like Nicholas to leave me without any word, and I worried about him. I knew he had become a diabetic, and had what he called his 'bad days', but when I consulted the Tarot on the matter the divination did not mention a passing. I traced a cousin of his, but he had heard nothing and presumed the worst. I knew of no one else to contact, so his fate still remains a mystery; I hope that one day it will be solved.

7 The Road goes ever Onward

I gradually became resigned to living on my own, and even started to appreciate it. In 1976 and 1977 I visited the Isle of Man at the invitation of the witches of Man, who said they were in need of advice on certain matters which they were sure I could supply.

I renewed my acquaintance with the witch Angus McCleod, who had known Gerald Gardner, and even looked like him. Angus was around the Witches' Mill and the surrounding buildings which housed Gerald's witchcraft museum, when the contents were sold, and the ballroom floor was strewn with a large mound of Gardner's letters and papers. The witches, Monique and Loic Wilson (to whom Gerald had bequeathed the museum) said, 'You can have them. Do what you like with them.' So he did; at Halloween Angus made a huge bonfire on the beach and, apart from certain items, burned the lot.

Angus presentd me with a very early *Book of Shadows* and other interesting papers that I was happy to have, because anything that had belonged to Gerald was of value to me. He also saved a beautiful illuminated book containing the Degrees of the Craft – a work of art, which he treasured. All personal correspondence was put to the flames.

There was another cry for help, soon afterwards. This time, from a member of my family. My cousin Alwyn died quite suddenly, and I went to Leatherhead to comfort his wife, Margaret. She was taking tranquillisers at the time, but it was not until much later that I learned she had collapsed and spent some time in hospital – the result of exceeding the prescribed dose.

I, too, was on stress-relieving drugs, and on my way home through London, via the Underground, my legs gave way near the bottom of an escalator, and there I was in a heap, with my luggage scattered around me. A stranger promptly pulled me to my feet and cleared the area of both me and my cases, averting what could have been a nasty accident. Had I remained where I was, the people coming down behind me would also have come to grief, with what might have been disastrous results.

I realized that I was taking too many tablets, and cut them down drastically, but not before another near-accident at Whitby. As I was driving along a narrow lane near the Abbey my brain seemed to switch off, and the car veered towards a stone wall. I recovered just in time and escaped having (at best) a badly scraped vehicle. Obviously the drug had adverse effects, so the rest of them went down the loo. Although I grew herbs and availed myself of their healing properties, I was far from being a 'whole' person at that time, and if the doctor prescribed something, I just went along with it.

I used to worry about my car in case it needed things doing to it, and I tried to keep it well and happy. The way I obtained it was very strange, and to relate the story I must go back to the year 1971, when Mother and I were taking some flowers to the family graves in City Road cemetery. As we approached the gates we passed several cars parked on the forecourt. One, a cream-coloured estate car with red upholstery and gleaming body-work, was extremely elegant. It caught my eye, and I exclaimed, 'How I wish I had a car like that one.'

We were needing to replace our car at the time and perused the advertisements in the local paper every night. I rang up about one of the vehicles advertised and was told it was still for sale. I asked where it could be viewed and, to my surprise, was told that the address was in City Road, directly across the road from us. When I called at the house in question the door was opened by an extremely handsome young man who took me to see the car, and, yes, it was the same one I had admired at the cemetery gates a few days earlier!

I could not quite believe that out of all the hundreds of cars advertised in that paper, I had hit upon that particular one, never dreaming it was for sale. Of course, we bought the car, and it gave us many years of service. I called it the 'White Goddess', as I believe that the Goddess had a hand in its purchase.

Adrian Burton, the car's previous owner, was on an exchange teaching scholarship from Australia and was soon to return home, so he wished to dispose of the car before leaving the country. Mr Burton was a regular reader of the *Sheffield Star*, and the following year an article by Sheila Tordoff, appeared in it, headed, 'The Witch Who Believes Divinity Is Chiefly Female'. The article included the story of my car, and how it came into my possession. Mr Burton wrote to Sheila Tordoff, relating his side of the story, which was duly published under the heading, 'Man who sold "The White Goddess" to a witch'. The relevant part of his letter, reads:

A Sheffield car dealer (who for diplomacy shall remain anonymous) answered the advertisement, and agreed to purchase the vehicle for a specified amount, and wrote out a cheque. Several days later I was informed that payment had been stopped on the cheque. When approached the dealer stated he no longer wanted the vehicle and he had no intention of paying for it.

My faith in human nature severely dented, I took possession of the vehicle again and re-advertised it in the *Star*. I received no immediate enquiries, and as I was under contract to return to Australia on a specified date I had unpleasant visions of having to leave an unsold vehicle as I winged my way homeward. I had almost given up hope of selling the vehicle, and my spirits were at a particularly low ebb when Mrs Crowther, who, fate would have it, also lived on City Road, phoned.

Our opposite individual needs were mutually satisfied. Her delight at obtaining a nice white estate car was equalled only by my delight at finding a buyer for my vehicle. Should you be interested to publish the 'down-under' version of The White Goddess, I would be appreciative . . .

The letter was signed, 'Yours sincerely, Adrian A.C. Burton, Deputy Headmaster, Keith Area School, Keith, South Australia.'

My profession often took me to Scotland, and during the long, solitary journeys my thoughts would drift into the past when my husband had accompanied me and shared the driving of the 'White Goddess'. On one occasion Arnold had taken me to the Burns museum in Ayr. It contained many of the poet's personal effects, including a mirror (or, as Burns would have said, 'a keeking glass'). For no reason I could think of, except perhaps vanity, I peered into the discoloured mirror, and a male voice with a strong Scottish accent resounded in my head: 'I see a lassie fair and kind, who would gi' all for peace of mind.' This was followed by another couplet of a more personal nature. I was alone in that room, as Arnold had wandered off, but I am sure that those words had been received clairaudiently. Had Robert Burns spoken to me as I gazed into his mirror? It certainly seemed so, and that bit about 'peace of mind' was very true, as I was always worrying about something or other.

In Scotland I met a young lady by the name of Fiona (a brilliant classical guitarist, she has since made many recordings and become famous). I stayed with Fiona, her husband and their three cats while playing Dundee; they lived in a nearby village in the thatched 'Froghoop Cottage, a charming olde-worlde abode.

Fiona took me to Arbroath (famed for its type of smoked haddock known the world over as the Arbroath smokie), where she knew of a sheltered cove outside the town.

A steep climb down led to a pebble-strewn beach entirely cut off from the seashore. Cliffs surrounded it, and the sea entered through a dark, cave-like opening in the rocks, the small wavelets creating a pool in a perfect magical setting. We filled our bags and pockets with pebbles of all shapes and sizes, so that our ascent to the cliff-top afterwards was heavy going. We needed lots of stones to make ourselves sets of runes, with plenty for other witches too. The things we do for England – sorry, Scotland!

We appeased our hunger with delicious fish and chips, eaten as they *should* be eaten: directly from their wrappings. Then we drove homeward at the end of a most enjoyable and rewarding day. That cove was so memorable that I included it in *The Zodiac Experience*, where it became Leon Dickens' illustration for the sign of Pisces.

On one visit to Scotland, some witches took me to see the Witches' Memorial, which is mounted on a stone wall facing the entrance to Edinburgh Castle. The bronze memorial is in the form of a small fountain with a rectangular trough to receive the water, although it has long ceased to function. Recently, when I was showing my American friend Eileen Smith round the city, we discovered that the memorial had been cleaned up and is now a tourist attraction! The legend above it reads:

> This fountain designed by John Duncan R.S.A., is near the site on which many witches were burned at the stake. The wicked head and serene head signify that some used their exceptional knowledge for evil purposes while others were misunderstood and wished their kind nothing but good. The Serpent has a dual significance of evil or wisdom. The foxglove spray further emphasises the dual purpose of many common objects.

The memorial is dated 1894, and side panels depict 'Healing Hands' and 'The Evil Eye'. I believe this is the only witches' memorial in existence, and for that reason alone is extremely important in historical terms. Clear evidence, if such were needed, of the untold horrors perpetrated on witches by Christian fanatics.

In Edinburgh I read of a very mysterious find on the hill called Arthur's Seat. In the summer of 1836 five boys were hunting rabbits on Arthur's Seat when the dog they had with them started scratching furiously at the hillside. One of the boys went to investigate and discovered what looked like the entrance to a tiny cave. He put his head inside – then quickly withdrew it, because it was full of tiny coffins. There were seventeen of them, arranged in three tiers; each one was four inches long and carved from a single piece of wood.

The boys immediately broke some of the coffins by throwing them at each other, but the next day had the presence of mind to show them to their schoolmaster, who just happened to belong to the local archaeological society. He prised the lid off one of them and was amazed to find a diminutive figure inside, carved in perfect detail. All the coffins held similar bizarre contents, and each figure wore what looked like male attire, i.e. tiny jackets and trousers.

Soon, Edinburgh was buzzing with the find, and even the *London Times* devoted half a column to the story. But was this an act of negative magic by someone who wanted these people dead? It certainly appeared to be sympathetic magic, in that by burying replicas of the people concerned, it was hoped to be rid of them. If so, was their aim achieved? We shall never know, but the coffins and their contents are on view in the Edinburgh Museum.

While in the 'Athens of the North', I decided to have a long evening kilt made in the MacFarlane tartan. (Arnold's mother was a MacFarlane, and as Arnold's widow, I was entitled to wear it.) I went to a very posh shop in Princes Street to be measured for it, and was asked which sett I required (there are three different tartans for that particular clan). The Hunting sett was lovely, all soft greens and blues, while the Mourning tartan was black and white, but I decided upon the Dress sett, which had a bright red background. I spent most of a week's salary on that kilt, but when it arrived, it was a most elegant garment and worth every penny.

In Scotland, the moon is known as 'MacFarlane's lantern', which I thought quite apt in the circumstances. The MacFarlanes were an extremely warlike clan who traced their descent from Gilchrist, of the ancient Earls of Lennox in the thirteenth century. The great-grandson of Gilchrist was named Bartholomew, and from its Gaelic equivalent, Parlan, the clan takes its name: MacPharlain, or MacFarlane.

Playing the Pavilion Theatre in Girvan, I stayed with witch friends in Dunure, a small, attractive fishing village a few miles south of Ayr. Dunure sports a famous optical illusion called the Electric Brae. When driving what you think is uphill, you are in fact travelling downhill, but an observer would swear the road went upwards. Gear-changing is quite a hazard on *that* part of the road.

A huge landmark on this stretch of coast is Culzean Castle, which was 'home' to President Eisenhower, during World War II. The woods surrounding the castle contain cedar trees, and I was given part of a fallen branch to take home. (Cedar, is one of the woods used when making the magical 'Fire of Azrael'.)

In the summer of 1977 I was again working in Edinburgh, and Ellen, a sister witch and High Priestess, gave me a Tarot reading. She said that I would meet a man who would become my future partner in life. A married man, he would already be interested in occult matters. I gasped, 'A married man? Oh no, he's not for me – no way!' Ellen, however, was quite adamant that our lives were due to be joined. I pointed out that it was unlikely to be the case if he was married. 'Oh yes,' she insisted, 'but he is not happy – his life is troubled.' Then she exclaimed, 'I think he has a Scottish name!' I let the matter rest; it would have been impolite to contradict my friend and most unwise to challenge the Tarot. Later that year, however, Arnold made himself felt with the news: 'You will soon be happy again, my darling, and in a very special way.'

In 1978 I received contracts to play Edinburgh yet again. It was then that I asked Ellen for a further reading. (I thoroughly enjoyed being the querent for a change – quite refreshing.) She spread the cards. 'That same man is here again, and you have now met him. As I said before, Pat, he has fair or reddish hair and blue eyes, and he is younger than you.' I thought, 'A young married man? Impossible!' Ellen smiled, 'There will be a lot of things for him to sort out, but he will certainly fall in love with you.' 'Oh dear,' I thought, 'why me?' My friend said I was not to worry as the Goddess would guide both of us. So many things had happened in which She had been the paramount factor. I would always be guided by the Goddess – and being a recipient of the Inner Mysteries made an even closer bond. So my faith in the future was as strong as ever. I left Edinburgh with a light heart and a stream of people going south for their holidays.

As I drove along, heading for the motorway, I noticed that a car which had previously overtaken me was just a little way ahead. The driver had obviously slowed down, so I passed him. A few minutes later the car appeared again, held back for a while, then passed me. Further on I saw that the driver had stopped in a lay-by, and soon after that he was once more on my tail. At one point I wondered, frivolously, if he was Ellen's mystery man, but as the game continued I began to get angry. What was he playing at? He stayed behind me until we hit the motorway, then passed, grinning and waving. Furious, I snarled at him and shook my fist. He got the message and streaked off into the distance.

I drove steadily for a while, recovering from the episode. I suppose a youngish woman with blonde hair, travelling alone, stands out a bit, and men, being men, will take any opportunity that presents itself to put another notch on their gateposts. All the same I was relieved that he had gone. I recovered my confidence, pressed down on the accelerator and really started to head for home. I thought of more pleasant things, such as Ellen's words – and pondered upon them.

She had said I already knew the man with whom I was fated to share my life. Who could it be? And was it possible that, after being on my own for four years, I had met this person – albeit unknowingly?

Since Arnold's passing, I had received proposals of one kind or another – usually from married men. One would-be lover came on the scene while my mother was still alive. I accompanied Joyce and John, an engaged couple, to a dance at the Conservative Club in Chesterfield. Most of the females turned up with partners, so John gallantly offered me a dance or two. Then, when I was sitting on my own, a very tall man approached and asked me to dance. Well, he really was a splendid dancer, and we whirled round the floor time after time. It was so good, as I had not enjoyed a dance for some years.

David was Irish, and held a responsible position in a large company. He called round one evening, and my mother and I made him welcome, but the hours dragged on and he made no effort to depart. It must have been well after eleven o'clock when I politely mentioned that it was time for my mother to retire. She excused herself, and when we were alone, David started to apologize, fervently. I asked why, as I had no idea what he was on about, and he said, 'Well, I cannot make love to you in your mother's presence.'

I stared at him, turned a giggle into a cough and quickly composed my features into a slightly puzzled look. 'I'm afraid you have got your wires crossed, David,' I said. 'I had no idea such a thing was on your mind.' He stood up, towering over me, an exceptionally handsome specimen, who now looked as though I had slapped him in the face. I made small talk as I led him to the door and wished him good night.

I had not given David any encouragement, except to invite him round, but he must have been anticipating a night of gay abandon. I'm afraid his ego was severely dented, and at the time I felt sorry for this, but I remembered a remark he made during the conversation, 'Oh,' he said, 'You are an *intellectual* woman,' as though it was some kind of rare disease; he seemed vaguely disappointed, as if an intelligent female was not in his line at all. I never saw him again.

One night, while staying at my cottage in Whitby, I had retired to bed in the 'Captain's Cabin', a small bedroom under the eaves, when in the darkness, a man's face appeared. It was a nice face, clean-shaven, with light, wavy hair, and it stayed for a few minutes before dissolving. Some time later, I received a letter from a man who lived in the stock-broker belt in Surrey, whose name was Clifford. (He was asking for some magic to be worked for him and in due course, it was performed.) I started to get very silly, thinking he might be the person I had 'seen' at the cottage – a big romance in the offing! Clifford rang to say the magic had worked, made charming conversation and filled my imagination.

I made another visit to see Margaret in Leatherhead, and it was there that Clifford came to see me. When I opened the door, I looked upon the face I had seen at the cottage, and just stood there gazing at him, before remembering my manners and inviting him in. I learned that Clifford's real interest in me centred on magic, and how his life and career could be further improved through it. We had already worked successfully for him, and I refrained from remarking that even a fairy only granted *three* wishes! And, yes, I also learned that he was a married man.

Clifford was very attentive and attractive, and during our conversation, I gleaned that he was not averse to the occasional fling. He smiled winningly and looked deep into my eyes, suggesting that he could come and see me in Sheffield. Despite being warmed by his compliments, I had no intention of furthering our acquaintance, and was aided in my resolve by Margaret's return.

When Clifford had gone, she exclaimed, 'What does he want with you, Pat? Isn't he a married man?' I enlightened her, and spoke of his interest in occult matters, and the subject was closed. In fact, that was the end of the incident. I did wonder, however, why I had a vision of someone who was to have such a brief impact upon my life. Perhaps Clifford had been thinking about writing to me at the time. Another Adonis – another damp squib!

At home, Ian Lilleyman, whom I had helped with a problem, called to see me. He was a quiet, somewhat shy person who had been kind enough to repair minor electrical faults that occur in a house from time to time. I regaled him with a cup of tea and my recent adventures, including the visit to Scotland and Ellen's reading.

'Who do you know with a Scottish name?' he asked, and I replied that I hadn't a clue. Of course, looking back on all this, the laugh was on me, because *Ian* was the man to whom the cards had referred – complete with his Scottish name. In those days, however, neither of us were aware of this. A further two years were to pass before we felt anything deeper than friendship between us, and by that time we were free to be together.

Looking back, we could see the accuracy of both Ellen's readings and Arnold's prophecy, but, as always, I continued to be amazed at the veracity of such pronouncements, even though I had had sufficient proof to last many lifetimes!

Ellen was also 'spot on' in the second reading, when she said I had already met this man. I had given a talk to the Sheffield Vegetarian Society, to which Ian belongs, and he was in the audience that night. We did not actually meet on that occasion, but a few months later, he said, he was worrying about a problem while staring through the window, when a voice inside his head said, 'Go and see Patricia Crowther.'

This led him to ring my door-bell one Saturday tea-time, asking if I could see him for a few minutes. Since I came into the Craft, requests for help have been common occurrences, but I was not too pleased at his unheralded appearance, because I was busy preparing for a meeting of the coven that night. My visitor looked so tired, however, that I finally invited him in and gave him a mug of strong tea and my attention for the next half-hour. After hearing him out, I said that I would consult the coven members on the matter and felt sure we could do something positive for him. As the dilemma was an environmental one, we eventually worked to create more peaceful conditions for him.

As Ellen had predicted, Ian was very interested in psychic matters and already possessed the entire part-work *Man, Myth & Magic*, an in-depth, well-produced encyclopaedia of the seventies, that built into several volumes. Arnold and I were featured in some of the many issues, and in 1968 Frank Smythe, who wrote the section 'Frontier of Belief', came to the Isle of Wight to interview us.

So for the time being, Ian slipped into my life, becoming a friend and someone who would always lend an ear to any troubles I had. This was a comfort, as even at that stage of our relationship, I knew I could trust him, implicitly.

After the publication of *Witchcraft in Yorkshire*, I was often invited to appear on Yorkshire Television, usually in their news programme, *Calendar*. I was nearly always interviewed by Richard Whiteley, and sometimes he would come to my house to record a piece which would go out the same day. One Samhain, there was an awful mix-up with tapes, and the recording failed to materialize. They apologized and explained that the gremlins had got into the works, so I was eventually shown the following October, when I looked a year younger.

One morning, Richard turned up on the doorstep with a camera crew, but without prior warning, which was highly unusual and inconvenient. I was totally unprepared, and after grasping that they wanted a piece on the May Day celebrations, I flew upstairs to slap on some make-up, gabbling to myself in the mirror to bring the relevant information into focus and cursing whoever was responsible for springing this upon me. I must say it was out of character, as requests to appear in the media were arranged by letter or by phone.

They required a short synopsis of the meaning of Beltane, to be filmed in an outdoor setting, so we drove to the nearby Norfolk Park. I was placed on a deserted path in front of the camera, then Richard introduced me, and I was on. I managed it on the first take by remembering part of an article

Clare and Alfred
Dawson (my mother
and father) some years
after their marriage in
1915. I was born
twelve years later

With my mother, smiling in
the sun. Photograph taken
in the Cholera Grounds
which overlooks the city of
Sheffield

As Prince Valentine in the
pantomime 'Goldilocks
and the Three Bears' at
the Theatre Royal,
Lincoln 1952–3.
I played the role of
Principle Boy for
many years

Skyclad in Gerald
Gardner's magic circle.
He used to say, 'In the
circle, female witches
usually wear a necklace
and a smile'

Gerald blessing us with the magic wand at my wedding to Arnold
Crowther. In occultism, the wand, among other things, symbolizes
the phallus and the sexual energy in a man and woman

A last picture with Gerald before leaving on honeymoon after my
marriage to Arnold Crowther, 9 November 1960

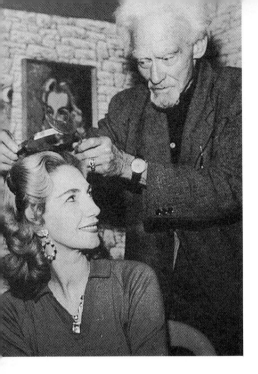

Posing in secular clothing for the *Yorkshire Post* several days after the ceremony proper in which Gerald Gardner crowned me 'Queen of the Sabbat'

Gerald Gardner outside the barn which adjoined his house *right* in Malew Street, Castletown, Isle of Man. The temple and the magic circle were on its upper floor. Access to it was gained through a small door in the bathroom of the house. There is a signpost on the wall which reads 'to the Witches' Mill'

'Seek the stone Sun
God's disc!'

At the unique witches'
memorial in Edinburgh,
designed by John Duncan
RSA in 1894 for the many
witches who were burned
at the stake near this site
on Castle Hill

The grave of Rupert Oswald Fordham in the churchyard at Highcliffe, Hants, where the ashes of Dorothy St Quintin Fordham (Gerald Gardner's friend and initiator) are buried

Gerald Gardner's witches' cottage at Fiveacres Country Club, Bricket Wood, near St Albans, as it looks today

The flame

With two famous authors at the Rollright Stone Circle: *right* Bob (R.J. Stewart) and Bill (the late William G. Gray)

Witch-priestess Kathy Billington at the Longstone, Isle of Wight.
The picture reveals a mysterious beam of light emanating from
the stone

I had written on the Beltane festival, a few weeks earlier. They seemed satisfied, and it came over quite smoothly on the box. Nevertheless, I would dread having to repeat that experience.

Richard Whiteley once asked me to read the cards for him. I saw a new position for him, and also a new programme. He was sceptical and said it could not happen, as he already had his position as a presenter. Time proved me correct, however. There were big changes in *Calendar*, and Richard went on to front the programme. He also presented a new word-game, *Countdown*, which has now run for several years. He featured in an afternoon chat show, and I was invited along one Hallowe'en, together with Chris Bray, from the Sorcerer's Apprentice bookshop in Leeds. It was a lengthy session, and a nice change to have another person on my side, so to speak. Between us, Chris and I effectively squashed unfair criticism of the Craft and easily prevailed.

Hallowe'en is always a busy time for me, and one year the director of the York Tourist Board wrote to ask if I would talk to a group of people who were pursuing a holiday which included visits to haunted houses and meetings with witches. He kindly offered to drive me there and back, so I accepted. At the Viking Hotel in York, my after-dinner speech, to guests arrayed in full evening-dress, resulted in a second invitation.

On that second occasion a gentleman well-known in York and elsewhere for an amazing supernatural occurrence he had witnessed was also speaking. His name was Harry Martindale. He regaled the avid audience, including myself, with this experience. It happened in 1953, when he was seventeen, and working as a plumber's apprentice. He was inspecting the cellar of the Treasurer's House in York. Almost as soon as he entered the cellar he heard the sound of a trumpet, and saw the head and shoulders of a man on horseback, appear through the walls. The man, who looked like a Roman legionary, was followed by around twenty Roman soldiers, tramping slowly behind him. They were bedraggled, dirty and unshaven, and their heads were bowed.

The soldiers were dressed in green leather kilts, roughly dyed, and carried round shields and long spears, with short swords suspended from their waists. One held a long, straight trumpet, much battered, and their helmets were decorated with fine plumes of undyed feathers. The rider wore sandals, cross-gartered to the knee, but the speaker said he could not see the soldiers' lower limbs, or those of the horse. It was as though they were travelling upon the surface of an old road *below* the floor of the cellar. They passed through the room and disappeared behind the opposite wall.

Unable to move, the young man's mind was busy challenging what his eyes had seen – and he had seen everything very clearly indeed. However, it was some time before he could come to terms with the apparitions, and even longer before he told anyone about it. Eventually, he admitted it to himself, and thought that the public should also be enlightened.

He found that there were inconsistencies between the uniform of a Roman soldier and the attire of the apparitions he had seen. The brass breastplate and the helmet topped with scarlet plumes, were absent, and the shape of the shields was different. Could these ghostly soldiers have been returning from an undertaking which had called for camouflage? A mission in which their ordinary uniform would have been too easily observed by an enemy? Were they indeed *Roman* soldiers? It is a very intriguing mystery.

Later that evening, as many guests as were prepared to go, dropped by the 'Cock & Bottle', in Skeltergate – an old inn reputed to be haunted. The story goes that the Duke of Buckingham's ghost frequents this watering-hole, and I positively refuse to make allusions to spirits of any kind.

I went along with the director of the Tourist Board, and he introduced me to Michael Aspel, the famous television presenter, who had been working in York, that day. Michael assured me that he had not suddenly materialized in the hostelry, and asked what I would like to drink. We chatted for some time, and I found him to be a charming man, completely lacking in airs; unlike some celebrities I have met!

Witchcraft appears to fascinate people from all walks of life. One speaking invitation came from the president of the Women's Institute, (if I remember rightly, it was the annual meeting of several branches of the WI in the Worksop area). I was introduced to the elderly Duchess of Portland, a patron of the society, before giving my talk, and for the meal I was seated as guest of honour next to the frail duchess. She asked me about the Goddess and seemed interested in my beliefs. Perhaps she was just being kind and polite, but I sensed a sympathy in her all the same.

Offers came in to lecture abroad, and one arrived from Spain. I was asked to represent British witches at the International Conference on the Occult Sciences, held at the Palacio de Congresos, de Montjuich in Barcelona, in December 1978.

As soon as I arrived at my hotel, the president and organizer, Felix Llauge Dausa announced that a hastily arranged press conference was to be held that same evening. I was hungry, not having had anything to eat since the in-flight meal, but we were taken to another hotel, where reporters and photographers were congregating. I was beginning to feel slightly light-headed, something that always happens when I am hungry and/or tired. (I had left home at five o'clock that morning, so it was hardly to be wondered at).

I noticed that the other lecturers were clutching notes, and I thought, 'I don't have any notes, but, so what! I can talk about the new Aquarian Age, and how this Age of Extension will broaden the understanding of such subjects as the Occult Sciences. This conference being a case in point! Yes, that will be fine – providing I can keep awake!' The fourth estate had a field day as we sat round a huge, polished table covered with microphones. Flashbulbs flared and died continually, and questions in a variety of languages filled the air. It was definitely an Aquarian-style event. Other speakers kept glancing at their notes, but I spoke off-the-cuff; sometimes this can be the best way – on that occasion, it was for me.

Afterwards, we were shepherded into another room where champagne and tiny sandwiches were laid out. My legs felt very strange and weak, and I could have wolfed all those sandwiches at one go, but there I was, sipping this champagne (really the last thing I needed in the circumstances) and chattering away to strangers, as if everything was fine. I met two people from England. John Cutten, an expert in psychic phenomena, and Bernard Davies, co-founder and senior secretary of the Dracula Association in Britain. I also met astrologers, clairvoyants, mediums and witches from different parts of the world. Most of them had a smattering of English, so we managed to communicate, if only at a basic level.

Just as I was dreaming of a lovely hot meal and a nice soft bed, Felix came over and introduced me to some television people from Madrid. They wanted me to appear on one of their programmes, in two days' time. There was much gesticulating and waving of arms, accompanied by excited Spanish voices, and I wondered, idly, if I could do the interview in bed. I could not imagine how everything could be fitted in, but it was all arranged for me.

The champagne was taking effect, and the scene around me receded into a rosy mist where nothing much mattered any more. My features became fixed in an artificial smile, as my glass was topped up with monotonous regularity. Just as I knew that I was about to disgrace myself by falling over, John and Bernard came to escort me back to the hotel. 'Good,' I thought, 'fresh air, taxi and food!' But, alas, the restaurant had closed. A solitary waiter said he would bring me something, but apparently, only fish and chips were left. One look at the plate was enough for me! The chips were burnt sticks, and the fish (dark grey, even black in parts) was oozing fat. I had never seen anything quite so revolting. I went to bed, on a piece of bread and a glass of water!

I was up early the next morning and among the first people down to breakfast. It was self-service, so I helped myself to everything in sight, but someone jogged my elbow and the tray crashed to the floor. Was there a conspiracy in Spain to stop me from eating? A new form of the Spanish Inquisition? I was luckier with the second tray and enjoyed my meal to the full. I'm afraid I am one of those people who fall apart without regular sustenance.

At the Palacio de Congresos we were ushered into a long room with an extremely low ceiling. It was already packed solid, and I started to feel a little claustrophobic, as there did not seem to be much fresh air in the room. Two speakers were to precede my talk, and I remember requesting the Goddess for more air and looking at the clock. Part of my lecture was to be illustrated, so I deposited the slides with the man in charge of the projector, gave him instructions, then sat on the platform awaiting the call of duty.

During the talk immediately before mine, there was some

discussion going on between Felix and two other men. I thought it was rather bad manners at the time but was too busy worrying about the projectionist, and whether he would handle the slides satisfactorily, to take much notice. When the speaker had finished, Felix came onto the stage, announced something in Spanish, and everyone got up and started to leave the room. Was there a fire? Then someone was kind enough to explain that we were going to the theatre ('What . . . now?'), that because of the size of the audience it would be better for everyone concerned if we changed to a larger auditorium. 'Thank you, Goddess,' I breathed, very glad to be vacating the executive suite.

We proceeded up a flight of marble stairs and entered the theatre. It was huge, with a wide stage, podium and large screen. We were requested to speak slowly for the benefit of the interpreters (the audience being equipped with the customary ear-phones). This was miles better – light and airy, and I felt comfortable in these surroundings. My talk received a standing ovation, and there followed a period for questions. I was then informed that both television and radio people wanted me in other parts of the building! I found these sessions very satisfying. The interviewers asked sensible questions, which gave me the opportunity to explain different aspects of the Old Religion.

After lunch, there was a nice surprise. Felix took me to a large department store and asked me to choose some gifts for myself. When we emerged, I was clutching some French perfume, a silk scarf and a Spanish-style hat.

On the flight to Madrid newspapers were distributed, and a picture on the cover of one of them caught my eye. 'That's a good one,' I thought, then, 'Good Goddess, it's me!' All the papers carried stories of the Conference. Television Madrid had booked me into a plush hotel, and there I stayed until the following afternoon. A pleasant oasis in a hectic three days, where I was soon enjoying a lovely, leisurely meal. I suppose I was lucky, being the only speaker chosen to appear on Spain's national television network. Once again, the Goddess had given Her aid!

Next day, I was whisked off to the television centre; fussed over in make-up, and finally ushered into a vast studio,

133

complete with studio audience. The presenter of the programme, José María Iñigo, was a charming person, and we had a little run-through before going live. I talked about the Cave of the Bats, discovered near Granada in the late nineteenth century. It contained the skeleton of a woman reclining in an inner chamber with her head resting upon her hand. She wore a robe of skins, a necklace and a diadem made from shells and teeth, and around her were other female skeletons, dressed in pointed caps and tunics. These lay in a semi-circle with the feet towards the 'queen', like the spokes of a wheel. They had carried exquisitely woven baskets of grain and poppy-seeds, which revealed the quiet manner of their deaths. In the passage leading to the cave, lay soldiers with flint knives, and a man who wore a simple gold headband. The cave was sealed from the outside and a Megalithic stone marked the entrance.

This discovery corroborates the evidence found at Sumer and elsewhere of the voluntary self-sacrifice by the 'queen' or priestess of the Old Religion for the benefit of the community as a whole. A sacrifice that also involved her retinue. Obviously this was a chthonic ritual of immeasurable age, later echoed in the Descent of Ishtar.

When I got back to Barcelona everyone had repaired to a Chinese restaurant. Meals seemed to be coming fast and furious now! Next morning, it was 'Home James', and with John and Bernard for company I sat in the departure lounge drinking coffee and talking nineteen-to-the-dozen. Our plane was delayed by fog at Heathrow, so it was a long wait, but after a time I noticed that the lounge had emptied. We had failed to hear the announcement of our plane's departure – it must have been given in Spanish! After all that waiting, we were the last passengers to board.

At home, I walked through the darkened rooms. It was quiet and empty. There was no one to whom I could recount my adventures, and the contrast after the activities of the last few days was unusually marked. But it was good to be back in familiar surroundings.

The next day I received a cable from Television Madrid, thanking me for my collaboration in their programme, 'Fantastico', and signed 'José María Iñigo'.

I caught up with John Cutten again, when I lectured at a three-day seminar for the Townswomen's Guild at Grantley Hall, near Ripon. In the course of it a group of us went to Fountains Abbey, where I wanted to see the carving of the 'Green Man'. The late Guy Ragland Phillips (one of the speakers), knew exactly where it was; he had done a lot of work on ancient sites, and was particularly involved with old churches that had been erected over pagan sites. His last work, *The Unpolluted God* (Northern Lights, 1987) is well researched, and a positive mine of information. It covers hundreds of old churches in which the Horned God is still carefully preserved.

When we arrived at Fountains Abbey, there was scaffolding on the part of the wall where the 'Green Man' is situated – high up, on one of the pillars – so it was hidden from view. John Cutten, who had brought his camera, was disappointed, as were all of us. Then, one of the workmen came over and asked John if he would like a photo of the carving. Would he just! So, taking the camera, our good Samaritan ran up the ladders, and obliged. Guy said how lucky we were to obtain a photograph at close quarters, when he had had to sketch it from the ground using binoculars, and indeed it was quite amazing good fortune to arrive on the day when that particular section of wall was being repaired. John was kind enough to give me one of the two photographs for inclusion in *Lid off the Cauldron*, which I was in the process of writing at the time.

Other notable events that final year of the 1970s included an appearance in *Afternoon Plus* for Thames Television with Mavis Nicholson, contributing to a Radio 4 series on witchcraft, *The Popular Image* (which also featured Robert Graves) and yet another slot on Yorkshire Television.

The decade had brought me many emotional tests and trials, so I hoped that with its ending, life would become more serene. However, 1979 gave me one last kick in the form of two red-haired men! A third man with similar colouring, made up the magical three, but he was an entirely different kettle of fish.

I noticed red hair because in ancient times people with this colouring were considered to be different, and set apart from the rest. Some were even sacrificed to the Old Gods. William II was a case in point. Surnamed Rufus, the Red Man, for his flaming locks, he was shot to death with an arrow in the New Forest by his bow-bearer, Sir Walter Tyrrel. This act was claimed by many to have been a Divine Sacrifice; a person, usually one in high office, being killed for the continued prosperity of the land and its people. The victim's blood had to run directly into the earth, and the fact that the body of the king remained in the forest, where it had fallen, until the following day, would seem to point to this vital prerequisite being fulfilled.

Two of these red-haired men were negative influences, although contact with both was very brief. The first appeared while I was giving a talk at the Grosvenor House Hotel in Sheffield to the staff of a building society. An auburn-haired young man constantly heckled me while I was speaking, but was told to keep quiet while the talk was in progress. At the end, however, he jumped up denouncing the Old Religion and behaving like a thing possessed. He could have been a Jehovah's Witness for all I knew, but it created a bad atmosphere.

I asked him to sit down and allow other people to put their questions, but he kept on ranting and raving, whereupon the room quickly emptied, and he finally walked out. His vehemence and obvious hatred were astonishing, and I wondered whether he had disrupted the meeting deliberately. Perhaps he had a tough time from the witches in a previous life – or had even been sacrificed to the Old Gods. The subject may have revived old memories from his subconscious. This sounds far-fetched, but such things *are* possible.

The second man with red hair was a veterinary surgeon – at least that is what it said on the plaque outside the door. This unhappy incident concerned the passing of Wiccan, a dear feline companion and a friend of Shah's.

I had arranged to take some friends of mine to the cottage for a week, and had planned to take Wiccan, too. She was thirteen years old, and something urged me to keep her close to me. Near to the time of departure my friends said there would not be enough room in their car for Wiccan's basket, so I took her to the cattery with Shah.

At Whitby a friend invited me round to read the cards for her, and, as she was interested in studying them, I showed her various methods of laying them out. Each time I did this, two cards came up. One was a card I always associate with a pet, and the other was 'The Tower'; the Tarot was telling me that one of my cats was in some kind of danger, but since I was not actually *reading* them, I failed to comprehend the warning. Had I done so, I would have gone straight home.

On my return, I headed for the cattery, to find Shah alone. A girl came and told me that Wiccan had started to cry out in the night, so they rang a vet, who gave her an injection to quieten her and took her to his surgery (this despite the fact that I had left them the whereabouts of my own vet, in case of any emergency).

I drove off in a terrible state, took Shah home and then went to find Wiccan. Rushing into the vet's surgery, I asked to see my cat and bombarded the receptionist with questions. Eventually, they brought Wiccan to me. She was only semi-conscious, and I nursed her and held her close. I was at my wits end.

When I saw the vet, he told me that she must have had a fit or a stroke, and there was nothing further he could do except put her to sleep. I could not think straight, so I sat in the corridor with her for quite some time, not knowing what to do. I wanted to do the right thing for Wiccan, but could not face the inevitable.

Although it was not our regular veterinary centre, where the excellent Mr MacTaggart was in charge, I had heard that this surgery was very good. So, what followed came as another shock. When the vet reappeared I thought I would collapse, but managed to ask him if I could hold her while he put her to sleep. He frowned and said sharply, 'Do you want to see her jump?' 'Jump?' I cried, 'why should she jump?' but he had already placed her on the table, and was feeling between her ribs.

Cur that I was, I blundered from the room. I heard her cry out three times, quite loudly, as he put the hypodermic syringe into her tiny heart. I am sure that is what happened. Why else would he feel between her ribs? And why did she cry out?

There had been times of anguish in the past when beloved pets were given a gentle, painless death in order to relieve their suffering, but they had passed through peacefully and instantaneously. I felt so terribly to blame to think that Wiccan, who had been so cherished by all of us, should be delivered up to such a heartless individual. Not knowing where I was going, I drove away with Wiccan's body beside me, then suddenly thought of Nicholas. Somehow, I reached him and poured out my sad story. As ever, he was the epitome of kindness, and the next day he buried Wiccan in the garden.

The third red-haired man was of course, Ian Lilleyman, a kind and deeply understanding person, with whom I eventually fell in love, and who helped to dispel some of the sorrow the decade had brought.

8　The Gifts of Venus

With the start of the 1980s I was in love again, and every-thing appeared brighter, yet subordinate to the person with whom I was emotionally involved. When Venus deigns to smile upon you, everyday tasks and anxieties recede before the all-enveloping radiance that sweeps you off your feet; at least, that is how it was for me. There was an exuberance that filled the mind and illuminated the whole being, so that the qualities of cheerfulness and hope sustained the spirit and supported the endeavours.

The most important of these endeavours was the writing of another book, *Lid Off the Cauldron*, published by Frederick Muller on 18 May 1981. This safe delivery of yet another 'baby' into the world brought feelings of both exhilaration and sadness. Seeing your work finally in print is good; it makes all the time spent in writing it well worth the effort. Yet, once the book is published, your 'baby' has been 'born' and gone out into the world, and this creates a feeling of sadness.

That month of May was memorable in other ways, too, principally because Ian and I were 'handfasted' on the 9th. We could have gone through a civil ceremony at a registry office, but we much preferred the older form of 'tying the knot' and receiving the blessing of the Old Ones.

Handfasting is an ancient ceremony of the Old Religion which binds two people together for as long as they are truly in love. It was outlawed by the Christian Church, which introduced the form of marriage that we know today, which binds a man and a woman together for life – in what some-times becomes hell on earth for the parties involved – and frowns upon divorce.

In Victorian times, the wife was mostly a breeding machine, breeding being the sole reason for marriage in the eyes of the Church. She had many children and often died, worn-out, before her time (my own grandmother had ten children and died in her forties). The husband, on the other hand, was free to have his mistresses and, if he was wealthy, would keep them in luxury in their own apartments. The Christian patriarchal system of belief turned a blind eye to these social misdemeanours. After all, the male sex was superior, and the Bible proclaimed that God was masculine! In terms of social injustice, hypocrisy and downright wickedness, the Victorian Age stands as a lesson to all women never to endure such humbug ever again.

In 1980 Ian had expressed a desire to become an adherent of the Craft, and he was already *au fait* with occult matters, generally. He went through the preparations necessary for all who seek initiation, including the obligatory waiting period of a year and a day.

This waiting period – which is often extended, as people differ in their comprehension of the Mysteries – benefits the Priest(ess) who will conduct the ceremony as much as the neophyte. Many things have to be considered, one of the most important being whether the neophyte has reached the required level of *awareness*. The inititator must be satisfied of the seeker's all-round suitability before taking such a serious step. It would be most unwise to initiate someone who failed to comprehend the implications involved (I speak from experience). Put simply, they should have reached a point in their lives when they truly feel the time has come to embark upon The Path: the quest for spiritual attainment and all-round growth. They should also have a deep longing within them to approach the Goddess and become one of Her Children.

It is said that nothing of lasting value is gained from a life of ease, and this is also true of the Mysteries. The Goddess watches you, and when She is satisfied with you, She will set things in motion. The truth of these words has been confirmed times without number by the Children of the Goddess.

Ian proved to be an apt pupil with a mind of his own, and

duly embraced the Mysteries with reverence and sincerity. Eventually, he was elevated to the position of High Priest of the Sheffield coven, and easily fulfilled his role. Initially a quiet, reserved soul, he blossomed into a commanding leader, extremely talented in the Magical Arts. Often I would stare at him, amazed by the transformation, but nonetheless jubilant at the progress he had made. Indeed, all the members of the coven commented upon Ian's competence, and the fact that this diffident, soft-spoken man became a vibrant and powerful priest in the 'Wood between the Worlds', as the Magic Circle is known.

Soon after our 'Handfasting', we went on holiday and visited several ancient sites in England, including the Rollright Stones, where I received an amusing and down-to-earth communication from the 'Whispering Knights', as usual put forth in rhyme.

At Mottistone in the Isle of Wight, we climbed up through the forest to the huge, solitary menhir called the Longstone that dominates the surrounding woods and valleys. (It was at the Longstone that a friend and priestess, Kathy Billington, had a photograph taken that, when developed, showed a sheet of white light appearing near Kathy's left arm, as if issuing from the stone. It was quite extraordinary.) Returning through the forest, we saw a dark shape hanging from a tree, directly over the path. Clouds of bees filled the air around this object, and I remembered flicking them away, earlier.

We realized that the dark mass was a swarm of bees and immediately made a detour to avoid it, moving quietly and without undue haste. Had the swarm been there when we scrambled up the path? It was something I had not previously encountered – all those bees making a single structure – a living cell! I recalled the link between bees and the Goddess, and how they often featured in religious iconography and matriarchal worship.

It was Ian's first visit to the Isle of Wight, so I took him to all the interesting sites, including Arreton Manor, a Tudor mansion that has a museum of children's dolls and toys on its top floor. I had visited it thirty years before with Arnold, and the curator had asked him if he could spare a puppet for inclusion in the display. Sure enough, it was still there, a

'Punch' puppet, with two others for company, among a varied collection of marionettes and dolls. Its label read: 'Punch puppet presented by Arnold Crowther, who performed at Shanklin Pier Casino and Puckpool Holiday Centre. This puppet has performed at Buckingham Palace (1939)'. It was an extremely odd feeling to see that puppet again after so long: it was as if part of life, frozen in time, was viewed from a long distance away. The puppet seemed to act as a key, unlocking memories which tumbled through my mind. It was almost as though they belonged to a previous life.

Our tour of sacred sites included those of the Avebury complex in Wiltshire (I wanted Ian to see as many of them as time would allow). Michael Dames' thought-provoking books on the area, *The Avebury Cycle* and *The Silbury Treasure*, cast a new light upon these ancient monuments. Silbury Hill, the largest man-made mound in Europe, is now thought to be the 'pregnancy' of the Earth Goddess. And the belief that the raising of the hill began in August, is confirmed by the winged ants (which fly in August) found in its core. This month, the Bron Trograin – the time when the Earth is in labour – was a most auspicious time for laying the foundations.

Excavations have revealed that the hill was constructed from various layers of turf, gravel, chalk and soil, and, deep at the base, a star-shaped pattern of double-stranded grass strings resembling a huge, three-dimensional spider's web. Echoes of Arachne? Some of the grass and moss within the mound was still fresh and green, and radiocarbon dating puts the raising of Silbury Hill at around 2660 BC, during the Neolithic period.

With the hill as the 'pregnancy', Dames suggests that the 'body' of the Goddess was formed by a moat that surrounded the base. This has long since dried up, but its shape is strangely similar to early statues of the Goddess, particularly that of the 'Sleeping Lady' from the Hal Saflieni hypogeum in Malta.

When he saw Silbury Hill, Ian was duly impressed. We had already decided to perform a rite on the top of it, and for a very special reason, so we returned there, after dark on a summer's night. Carefully negotiating the wire fence at the hill's base, we climbed the steep slope and found our way to the central 'eye' indentation at the top. We were halfway through the ritual, when we suddenly heard a deep , masculine voice – laughing in the darkness. We immediately dropped to the ground; then, hearing nothing else, we got up and walked to the edge of the hill, our torches probing its sides. They were deserted; there was no sign of another living soul. We waited, listening intently, but nothing disturbed the windless night air. We concluded the ritual, gave wine as a libation, and quietly left the site.

In the car, we talked it over. The voice had seemed so *near* us – a sudden explosion of mirth. If a human agency had been responsible for it, we would certainly have seen the person departing down the hill when we shone our torches on the smooth slopes. From this, we deduced that the laughter had come from an entity drawn there by the ritual. Who knows, our invocations may have awakened an ancient god-form from that area. Months later, I came across a reference to Silbury Hill in a library book about haunted places. The writer stated that close by the mound there was a spot which was known locally as 'Pan's Place'.

In 1981 we received an invitation to attend a lavish party for occultists at the Savoy Hotel, London, on 18 October. The event was arranged by Mr and Mrs Carr P. Collins Jr, from Dallas, Texas, along with Mr and Mrs Desmond Burke and Miss Victoria Neeves. A real Venusian occasion!

Carr Collins was the initiator of the 'Sangreal Foundation', which published books on the cabbala and related subjects. He was a tall, tanned and very attractive person whose aesthetic qualities were apparent to all who met him. Some years before meeting him at the Savoy, I had seen Carr clairvoyantly, while reading the Tarot for Bill Gray, and I had a clear vision of this person who was to become a prominent figure in Bill's life. As with Clifford, it was very strange to meet someone after this – to actually see them in the flesh, so to speak. It was also exciting, and confirmed the accuracy of the visions.

I met many old friends that day including Basil Wilby, formerly editor of *New Dimensions*, an excellent occult publication. He reminded me of the time when Arnold sent him ideas for articles, scribbled on old cigarette packets. I also met the author, Israel Regardie, who was once secretary to Aleister Crowley. All in all, it was a marvellous day.

It was repeated in 1983, when Collins extended his largesse at the Goldsmiths' Hall in London. That day, my friend, Bill Gray was present, although it was to be the last time we would meet in this lifetime. Israel was absent due to ill-health, but I recalled my last glimpse of him at the Savoy, talking to Carr in a window-seat with the setting sun shining upon them. I remember this, because a few years later, they both passed away within a short time of each other. There were also some witches at Carr's party who had belonged to Gerald's St Albans coven and whom I had met all those years ago at Fiveacres covenstead. It was most enjoyable to see them, and I much appreciated meeting Carr Collins and his lovely wife Lucia again.

One Hallowe'en, BBC Radio Wear, based in Middlesborough, invited me for a lunch-time slot. During the programme several occultists rang in, and for once there was an absence of irate Christians. Whether this pleased Radio Wear or not I had no idea, but I enjoyed every minute of that broadcast. A lecture in York the same day was a different story. Once again the venue was the Viking Hotel, but this time I was speaking to the staff of a department store in the city. To this day I am not sure what they expected of me; they probably thought I would enthrall them with the usual sensational stories of Black Magic, not to mention a sex orgy or two. I had an uneasy feeling as I waited in the bedroom, and the two girls who came to say they were ready for me gave me the distinct impression that they were expecting some kind of titillation. They smirked, knowingly, at each other, so that I felt decidedly apprehensive as I walked downstairs to my doom.

In the ballroom, a table stood on the dance floor, with the people sitting in semi-darkness. There were off-putting noises from the bar at the back of the room, which did nothing to aid my confidence. When the audience grasped the essence of what I was saying, and realized that there were to be no sensational revelations, my talk was endured in a sullen uninterested silence. I invited questions from the floor, and some of the more daring souls revealed their interest in the Dennis Wheatley variety of magic, which confirmed my previous fears. I corrected false impressions, and that did nothing to enhance my popularity.

Another, happier engagement in York was again at Hallowe'en, and was preceded by an interview with Molly Price-Owen, for the BBC World Service. Both events were a big improvement on that last visit.

Speaking of the darker side of the occult, I recall something which occurred one year, after our Samhain celebrations. Everyone had gone home, and I was relaxing with a mug of hot chocolate, before retiring. The house was very quiet, and suddenly I heard an unearthly growling noise at the back door. The mug stilled halfway to my lips, and the cats, which had been sleeping peacefully in front of the fire, shot awake, their attention focussed in the direction of the noise. I am not easily frightened, but whether it was the unexpectedness of the sound or my psychic senses picking up hostile vibrations, my skin crawled.

I walked into the kitchen, and the cats, creeping stealthily behind me, stared at the door, their tails like bottle-brushes. Something was on the other side of the door. A dog – or. . .? If it *was* some kind of malignant spirit, why did it not pass *through* the door? My house, unlike other dwellings was a covenstead where prayer and ritual had been constantly performed for many years; the very building must to some extent be permeated with positive vibrations. Were these a barrier to whatever lay outside? Nevertheless, I decided that a 'dismissal' would not go amiss and, snatching a knife from the drawer, I performed the 'Banishing Pentagram', bringing my will to bear upon what lurked beyond the door. I felt angry now, and that helped.

Nothing more was heard, and when I peered through the curtains the yard appeared to be empty. (Of course, whatever made the noise need not have had a material form, but I had a look, anyway.) The cats returned to their places by the fire, so I took that as a good sign and hoped the owner of that ghostly, hideous noise had departed whence it came.

Before the disturbance, I had thought of taking some

rubbish out to the bin, as I often potter about last thing at night. For some reason, though, I had decided to leave it until the morning. If I *had* gone out, would I have encountered whatever it was that came to the door? The behaviour of my cats alone informed me of the presence of something malevolent, and I felt certain that no living creature could have been responsible for what we had heard.

Incoming mail regularly included letters for help. One arrived from a lady who wanted to know if I would cleanse her home of any unwelcome vibrations that might be present. The house had been on the market for quite some time but she had been unable to sell it. She seemed to think that this was due to its being jinxed in some way.

I had met the lady some weeks previously, when I performed a Tarot reading for her, so I agreed to perform a cleansing ritual at her house, and purify it, generally. It was a large, detached property containing fifteen rooms, and I repeated the ritual in all of them. The entire exercise took about three hours and afterwards a copious amount of vital *élan* had gone off me, so my hostess regaled me with cups of tea and home-made apple pie.

In one of the rooms, I had 'seen' an old gentleman in a rocking-chair, but there were no bad vibes from him. The lady said that the room had belonged to her late father, who had always sat in his rocking-chair towards the end of his life. She agreed that her father's spirit was unlikely to be against her selling the house.

Two days later, she rang to say that she had sold the house and was amazed how soon after my visit this had occurred, considering that the property had been on the market for almost two years. 'My dear,' she exclaimed, 'you really are the best of witches!'

Successes like these are encouraging, but should never lead to over-confidence. That can be a fatal error and is one of the reasons why so many occultists fail in their quest. Unless you realize that you are only a channel for the higher powers, and not 'Lord High Everything Else', failure is inevitable. Certainly, the soul improves through transcendental experiences, but the sole criterion of The Path lies in the words, 'I wish to learn in order to serve'.

I am always fascinated by life's achievers, and Rod Powell is one of them. He is a very fine sculptor from Sheffield who received a commission to carve a figure of his own choosing in the city's Graves Park. Rod decided to make his figure, one of a series of art-forms in the park, depict the Green Man. He spent weeks standing on a ladder against a tree, working at the top of the trunk, but, the finished work was wonderful. There was the Green Man, sitting high up amidst the foliage with his arms encircling the tree and his antlered head outlined against the sky. He joins other gods featured in the city. Vulcan stands on the topmost pinnacle of the Town Hall, while Mercury is similarly placed on the Sheffield Star newspaper offices.

I have visited Stonehenge on numerous occasions, but my work has always prevented me from being there at the Summer Solstice. Changes in my life, now made it possible, however, so Ian and I took a vacation at the appropriate time of the year.

A Stonehenge Summer Camp was situated across the road from the monument – the 'Hippies' were there in force! We were warned that it would be unwise to go as 'anything could happen on the longest day', but were unable to find out exactly what this warning meant. I said to Ian, 'We *will* go, and if there is trouble of any kind, we can always leave.'

We arrived at about two in the morning on the day of the Solstice. A man was standing in the road directing vehicles into a field car-park, and it was very quiet. Eventually, people from the camp began drifting across to the stones in twos and threes, and we joined them. There was still an hour to sunrise.

The stones loomed large above us as we wandered between them, or stood absorbing the atmosphere and waiting for the sun. The Druids appeared and performed rituals among the stones, which made for a deep, contemplative mood among the hundreds of souls now gathered there. The sky was lightening, but a curtain of thin cloud obscured the sun's disc, which was visible as a pale, diffused beam of light. By this time, everyone had formed into a long line immediately behind the Hele Stone, so that its faint shadow would cover them.

One or two young men were actually sitting on the top of the trilithons. Of course, it was this sort of activity that induced the authorities to forbid entry to the stones ever again. That year, 1984, was the last time the public would be allowed the privilege. How lucky we all were to have been there on that particular day!

At Stonehenge on the Summer Solstice a very special and wonderful thing occurs, which although it is part of the pattern of the place, is not common knowledge. When the sun rises on that day, it is seen to 'sit' upon the Hele Stone, but the real mystery at Stonehenge is enacted while the sun is rising and *before* it reaches the top of that stone. As the sun lifts over the horizon, the *shadow* of the Hele Stone begins to creep over the grass, and finally enters the circle. The sacred Marriage of Heaven and Earth is proclaimed at Stonehenge when the phallic shadow of the Hele Stone enters the circle-womb of the Earth Mother – a sacred marriage indeed!

So our visit turned out to be a satisfactory and spiritually rewarding experience, during which we praised the brilliant engineering capabilities of our ancestors. They it was, who generated a breadth of vision and a view of cosmic unity we would do well to emulate.

I feel contented when I am wandering round sacred sites; they are, after all, an important part of our heritage. Today they are coming into their own, thanks largely to special people with minds unclouded by religious prejudice. Stonehenge is a case in point. This monument has received expert attention from Professor Gerald Hawkins. In *Stonehenge Decoded*, he explains that by means of modern technology he discovered that the Hanging Stones were built as a stone calendar. He found that they were aligned to the sun's and the moon's risings and settings throughout the year. Stonehenge thus unifies astronomical and religious concepts into a harmonious and unique at-one-ment. It is not alone in this, as other stone circles and avenues follow the actions of the heavenly bodies in a variety of alignments; each with its own form of expression.

Moving from the sublime to the ridiculous, an amusing incident occurred around this time, at the hairdresser's. A vicar came in and sat in the chair next to mine. (I believe he was having a trim). There we were, a witch and a Christian priest sitting side by side, having their hair done! The times, they are a-changing!

There were always letters on the door-mat, and one came from a European Princess, who shall be nameless. She wanted to see me urgently on a very important matter, but would prefer to tell me about it, face to face, in case her letter went astray. Intrigued, I replied, suggesting a suitable date and time, and when the young lady arrived, her chauffeur drove discreetly away and left us together.

She was young and very pretty, with dark hair, large, lustrous eyes and an hour-glass figure. She chattered away over the refreshments I provided, and eventually disclosed her secret. She was in love with a Prince of the British Royal Family, and wished to marry him. She was absolutely certain they were meant for each other, although they had met only once or twice on social occasions. If she could not have him, her life would be destroyed. These words were uttered with intense feeling, and tears welled up in those marvellous eyes.

When faced with the emotional problems of another human being (as has often happened since I entered the Craft), my Libran detachment comes to the fore. I do not mean that I am lacking in sympathy, but I instinctively identify with the figure of Justice, holding the Scales of Balance. After all, if I were overwhelmed by the unhappiness of another, I would be helpless to aid them at all! Therefore I must always invoke Maat and offer compassion combined with commonsense, regardless of how I am viewed by the person who confides in me.

I found out that my visitor was a Roman Catholic and, at the risk of another emotional outburst, explained very gently that, even if the Prince fell violently in love with her, he would not be allowed to marry a person of her religious persuasion – at least, I strongly doubted it. She was silent for some minutes, then said that she had never considered, or even thought of *that* particular obstacle.

From her conversation, it appeared that her acquaintance-ship with the Prince had been of the shortest duration. He had talked with her, and they had apparently enjoyed each other's company at public functions; on one occasion, she had been invited to Buckingham Palace, but that was all. I deduced, without much difficulty, that the light of her life had merely been acting towards her as public figures do: functioning at the level of etiquette required on social occasions. In other words, he was playing his part. And what man could be blamed for gazing deeply into those liquid eyes. . .?

I had to let the Princess down gently, so I explained that even if he *had* been available, it was not within the jurisdiction of the Craft to compel anyone to fall in love against their will. She had heard about love spells and such and thought that I could suggest one for the Prince. I had to say that I was unable to fulfil her desire in this and, even if I had been willing, I would hesitate to do so, because I was not keen to be locked up in the Tower of London.

I did not want to lead her into any further distress, so I suggested that she could work a spell herself, although the best ones required the proximity of the beloved, at least for a while. I could have been mistaken but I suspected that, being a princess, she obtained most of the things that she wanted in life. Young men must surely have been attracted to her, both for her looks and her vivacity. I promised that I would work some magic for her to find emotional happiness, but that was as far as I was prepared to go.

She said she would write, and departed in a more serene frame of mind than when she arrived. I worked my magic for her, and in a few weeks, received the gift of two kaftans – one white, the other green, the fairy colours. An unexpected, but welcome surprise.

On Christmas Day 1986, when my cat Shah was fourteen years old, cousin Sheila gave me a large, black ceramic cat as a present. As soon as I opened the parcel, I knew that Shah would pass over within three months. I felt sick, but smiled and kissed my dear cousin; she was not to know that her gift was also a warning. Shah was killed on the road three months later. There were no marks on his beautiful black coat, apart from a tiny scratch on his neck. I was inconsolable for a long time, for Shah had also been the last link with Arnold and my Mum.

After that, I needed to be alone for a while. Jessie, however, was a very old friend, a priestess herself, and very understanding. I could pour my heart out to her, and I knew that what I said would go no further – that, to me, is a true friend and the only kind worthy of the name. Jessie read the Tarot for me. Her deck showed the 'Queen of Wands' with a black cat at her feet, and this card came out in the reading. 'Look,' Jessie exclaimed, 'that's your mother, and Shah's with her.' – Which could have been perfectly true. The Goddess also appeared in the spread, with the Ace of Cups, a card meaning among other things Birth or Rebirth. The Goddess was showing me a renewal. A kitten, another cat? I did not feel well enough to go out and look for one, but then you do not have to search for the Gifts of the Goddess, they arrive of their own accord.

I began to notice a tortoiseshell cat who came into the garden occasionally, stayed awhile, then left. One day she arrived heavily pregnant, then I did not see her for many weeks. I was curious to know about her, and tried to follow her to find out where she lived. Two roads away I lost her, so I enquired at the nearest house. I was told that one particular dwelling had lots of cats which were always in kitten.

Jessie called at the house in question, but before she could utter a word the woman said. 'Do you want to see the kittens? I keep them in the wash-house.' Jessie was shown four cardboard boxes full of kittens, and was told, 'I have four Queens, and they are always in kitten. I sell them at the market.' The house was dark, and stank of unmentionable things. Jessie thought, 'Perhaps they are better off in the wash-house' and could not wait to get away.

Did some of those kittens belong to the tortoiseshell? If so, she did not have them for long! I was disgusted. To think that anyone could allow four cats to have continuous litters for such small commercial gain. I kept an eye on that house, and one day I saw the tortoiseshell cat run through the gate.

The little cat's visits to me gradually lengthened, although I never fed her and I kept the door open so that she could depart whenever she felt the need. One evening she looked at the open door, then jumped onto a comfy chair and went to sleep. Had her kittens been sold? She was certainly not her usual perky self. I was not unduly worried about the rights and wrongs of the situation, now that I knew the conditions under which she had lived. I called her 'Twinkle', because after Shah's death she brought a twinkle of light into my life, and was so very loving.

There was the Tarot reading, too. This was borne out at the Summer Solstice the same year, when Twinkle became an expectant mother yet again. Her three jet-black kittens were born in my wardrobe, and I thought of the words of the Goddess; 'I give back three-fold, that which I take!'

Daddy-cat was a black stray, but often called to see his offspring, and have a good meal at the same time. He would not come into the house, so I fed him in the garden.

Kittens had never previously been born in my home, and it was very exciting. There were two males and one female, the latter an independent little soul who eventually went to live a life of luxury with Ian's Mum and Dad. I named the males Tam Lin and Shah II and in many ways Shah's character is very like that of his namesake. Perhaps for the first time in her life Twinkle was able to keep her kittens and watch them grow, and she was a very good mother too.

I believe that the Goddess also looked after Twinkle, for she lived a life of ease with us for nine years until a swelling was diagnosed as a malignant tumour. An operation failed to improve the situation, as the growth had penetrated into Twinkle's lungs and she had spasms when she struggled to breathe, which could not be allowed to continue. Twinkle found peace at home in her comfy chair. The lady vet and her female assistant were in attendance, while I lovingly held her. Three women, expressing the compassion of the Threefold Goddess.

It was in the 1980s that an attack upon all aspects of the occult erupted in Britain, in the wake of a similar onslaught in the USA. It was instigated by Christian fundamentalists in order to create hysteria and fear, and sensational reports soon flooded the media alleging the abuse of children by followers of cults – not least those of witchcraft! Fundamentalist leaders promulgated the idea of satanic ritual abuse; a term which, at that time, became synonymous with the occult and/or the vaguest hint of any misdemeanour in which children were concerned.

To the Christian fundamentalists the Devil exists in a

personified form and will attack or possess any person who does not subscribe to biblical writ. Fanaticism of this kind put one in mind of the religious fervour that gave birth to the Spanish Inquisition and was behind the persecutions in the sixteenth and seventeenth centuries, when Europe's skies were blackened by smoke from flames that consumed the living bodies of men, women and children. It was difficult to comprehend, though, that in this so-called Age of Enlightenment many people swallowed such arrant nonsense hook, line and sinker.

The Social Services were targeted as the people who must be on their guard and chase the Devil wherever he reared his head. Fundamentalist scaremongering left a trail of misery in its wake, not least as a result of the abduction of children by social workers, snatched from their parents in the dead of night, as took place in the Orkneys and in Rochdale, Lancashire.

Sensational reports flooded the press, and television programmes cobbled together from odd bits of film vaguely connected with occultism or Black Magic, were regularly featured. Born-again Christian women were interviewed and said they had become ensnared in covens and witnessed the rape of virgins or the sacrifice of an infant, yet had failed to report the crime to the police. What is more, they went back at other times for more of the same – or so they said.

The Devil, of course, was an invention of the Christian Church, and is part of the Judaeo-Christian belief system. Therefore, this bogey man is entirely the responsibility of those who brought this horrendous thought-form into existence. And as with all such thought-forms, it is now in the process of turning upon its creators. The Old Religion, by contrast, has no figure representing personified evil. Its teachings assert that, although men and women are born with both positive and negative traits, they also have *free will*. Whether they realize it or not, the way in which they choose to conduct their lives, affects their spiritual evolution, for good or ill.

This doctrine is exemplified in the witches' creed: 'An' it harm none, do what ye will.' Such positive counsel is of the utmost importance to followers of The Path, and those who practise magic. The creed tells you that no one must be harmed through your actions or as a result of your magical work. Even though you are performing magic for the most altruistic reasons, you must follow it through, and try to discern what its impact may be upon those *indirectly* affected by the results. The admonition 'Do what ye will', does not mean 'go and do what you feel like doing'; it emphasizes that you must *recognize* and *perform* your true will; something that requires deep thought. Comprehending the creed raises further questions about Selfhood – 'Why am I here?' 'What must I do?' and these questions can best be answered through the study of your birth-chart.

One man to whom credit must be given for his tireless and energetic defence of occultists generally is Chris Bray of Leeds. He engineered a most important service, known initially as the Sorcerer's Apprentice Fighting Fund, which stood forth to safeguard freedom of belief against cultural ignorance, prejudice and downright untruths. Chris's prolific output, aided by an undoubted talent and expertise in the field of the spoken and written word, was used to excellent effect when dealing with the media. Established in most aspects of occultism and magic, and an adherent of the Craft to boot, he would rapidly burst the paranoid bubbles of the fundamentalists and was in touch with officialdom in all its forms.

Bray's regular and informative news-sheets were distributed in pagan circles and provided readers with the latest forms of attack, so that they were able to defend themselves and their beliefs. Often immediate action was necessary. A case in point was a shop in Lincoln which the local council was thinking of closing down. The owners had already had their windows broken, and when they moved to new premises they were fire-bombed. These offences were the direct result of the fundamentalists' campaign. The shop stocked innocuous items, such as Indian ware, jewellery, candles, incense, etc, and provided the owners' livelihood. Many people, including myself, rang the Council chambers at Lincoln to protest at the outrage, and the idea of closing the shop was dropped like a hot coal. But for the adroitness of Chris Bray, it would have been a different story. Everyone concerned owed him a debt of gratitude for organizing a project which eventually led to this particular and prolonged 'witch hunt' being well and truly squashed.

To aid their campaign, the fundamentalists attempted to recruit people close to government. One of these was the late Geoffrey Dickens, MP for Littleborough and Saddleworth. In April 1988 he called for a debate on witchcraft in the House of Commons and said that offences were being committed against children in occult ceremonies. He warned the House that witchcraft was 'sweeping the country', but his statement was greeted with jeers of derision, and the House dissolved in cat-calls and hoots of laughter. I was watching this particular session, and remember it well. I could imagine the reactions of one MP, a friend of mine, who was well acquainted with my beliefs!

I immediately wrote to the Home Secretary, explaining the ethical and moral content of the Old Religion, and that I was deeply offended by Mr Dickens' unwarranted and inaccurate remarks. I pointed out that I had yet to learn of any genuine adherent of the Old Religion being apprehended for breaking the laws of the land in any way whatsoever, and commented that it would seem there were the good and the not so good in most religions, unless criminals were either atheists or agnostics.

Geoffrey Dickens continued his crusade, and on 7 October 1988 I was asked to appear with him in a television programme, the *James Whale Radio Show*, along with Monseignor Michael Buckley, the religious adviser for Yorkshire Television. The producer of the show requested a short ritual, so we decided to bless the wine and dedicate it to the Goddess. This was filmed in the foyer of the studios. I then carried the chalice along a passage and into the studio, while a cameraman walked backwards in front of me – not easy, as the floor was covered with masses of thick cable, but I managed it without tripping or spilling the wine.

What I did not know at the time, was Buckley's reaction to the ritual. While Ian and I were out of the studio, James asked him what he thought of it, and Buckley growled, 'Bah! theatricals!' Ceremonial, of course, *is* acting, and is intended to raise the consciousness of the participants. It is no good just standing there and muttering to yourself, or handling artefacts as though you were cooking in the kitchen. The Monseignor's comment was very sour grapes.

The programme also featured filmed interviews with occultist Brenda Brandolani, the Rev. Kevin Logan and Chris Bray. Chris was also on the phone-in of that show, and tore strips off Dickens. The MP had said he would not appear if Bray was invited into the studio. What was he afraid of?

Dickens boasted that he had a briefcase filled with incriminating documents against occultists, but he later claimed it had vanished – in any event, it never came to light.

A minor contretemps occurred in the Green Room, before the programme. Geoffrey Dickens and his lady companion were sitting opposite to me when he suddenly asked, 'Do you eat babies?' I gasped, 'Are you for real?' I then remembered Aleister Crowley's reply to the same question – 'Yes, but only the very best,' but thought better of using it; a facetious reply would be taken literally. Dickens went on, 'Is the Devil present at your meetings?' I retorted, 'Well, I haven't noticed your presence, there!', whereupon he shut up. I really could not quite believe what I was hearing. For a supposedly responsible Member of Parliament to ask such puerile questions was incredible. Was he into the novels of Dennis Wheatley?

There was yet another appearance for Yorkshire Television in a new series *Cat Calls* – all about cats. When the presenter, Rob McBride, and several technicians came to my home to film the piece I did not imagine that any of my three cats would also take part. Shah and Tam Lin were extremely nervous of strangers, and strangers with boxes, wires and lamps would be enough to frighten them out of their fur coats. However, just before my visitors arrived, Twinkle (Shah and Tam Lin's mother), came into the room and perched herself on the arm of a winged chair. I was pretty sure she would vanish when they appeared and forgot about her in the subsequent flurry. When all was ready for filming I suddenly noticed that Twinkle was still sitting on the chair, even though it had been moved to another position. So during the recording she sat beside me; she was even given a close-up and looked the camera straight in the eye, as though

156

she enjoyed every minute of her fame. Twinkle was a star!

Rosemary Guiley, the American author, wrote to me requesting profiles of Arnold Crowther and myself for an in-depth encyclopedia on witchcraft she was in the process of writing. I was also able to supply her with details on the background of Gerald Gardner, which she regarded as being relevant in building a comprehensive biography of him. Guiley's prodigious work was published in 1989 as *The Encyclopedia of Witches and Witchcraft*.

Hard on the heels of this project, came another. The author Howard Rodway asked me to design three Major Arcana cards for a new Tarot deck, *The Tarot of the Old Path*, published in 1990. Rodway, who wrote the book for this Tarot, also requested a verse on the subject. Strangely, before I received his letter several lines of poetry about the Tarot had popped into my head in the middle of the night. So I already had a basis for the verse. (What you might call convenient clairvoyance!) This new deck featured concepts, symbols and imagery drawn from the Old Religion, and as Howard states in the introduction to the book '. . . in recognition of the many card readers who are witches and initiates of Wicca, otherwise known as the Old Religion, the Craft of the Old Path.'

The cards I designed were, 'The Sun', 'Judgement' and 'The World'. As soon as I received the request images for these cards began crowding into my mind, but the one known as 'Judgement' worried me, because of its Christian bias. The idea that one is judged after death, by the Judaean-Christian god, is anathema to pagans, and depends heavily upon the morality and teachings of Christianity. Should a person lapse, there is the promise of punishment, of being burned for eternity in the 'Fires of Hell'. Pagans know well that during the persecutions fires were certainly lit upon the Earth. The Church considered that the agony of being burned alive might perhaps save the soul from that fate in the after-life – and by this method, it was also able to rid itself of thousands, if not millions, of people who for one reason or another resisted its authority and power.

I thought of the teachings of the Old Religion, especially of being responsible for one's own soul – a concept enshrined in the belief in reincarnation. The idea that for every action (good or bad) there is an appropriate reaction: the Law of Karma. Thus, as it journeys through life after life, the soul is continually brought to face its weaknesses, until the negative traits that prevent its progress in Cosmos are eliminated and gone for ever.

In light of the above, the 'Judgement' card became 'Karma', and, as the Law of Karma penetrates all Planes (its final resolution being that of godhood), I began the task of designing a picture, portraying these Inner Planes.

So far as our minds are able to comprehend the *nature* of the Planes, they appear to be composed of the inner, or spiritual qualities of Water, Air and Fire. (There is little doubt that more ethereal dimensions exist beyond them, of which humanity as yet, knows nothing.) I realized that even today the vast majority of people in the Western world are still ignorant of these after-life conditions or soul-states. Memorials to those who have passed over that contain the words, 'sleeping', or 'at rest', give some idea of what is believed to occur after the death of the physical body: in a word, nothing! You 'go to sleep', and you jolly well stay asleep! Some people have a vague idea about a place called 'Heaven', where the soul dwells for ever in bliss, but nothing more than that.

When you consider that all schools of learning were closed in Western Europe during a period which became known as the Dark Ages and that a mere hundred years ago many people were still unable to read or write, it is no wonder that esoteric subjects were considered to be far above the heads of the common people. Today, however, the Christian Church is gradually losing its hold over the minds of men and women, and the shining Lamp of Knowledge and Enlightenment illuminates the darkness.

Although *diagrams* describing the Inner Planes have occasionally appeared in literature, I believe the 'Karma' card is the first portrayal of the Inner Planes to be published in a pictorial form and it was through the talents of Sylvia Gainsford that a glimpse of them was brought into being. Sylvia, as one would expect of a British Academy artist, executed the 78 cards brilliantly, and brought her own special gift for painting birds and animals to many of the cards. For the record, 'The Tarot of the Old Path' is now the most popular Tarot in the States, and the seventh most popular in the world. Sylvia informs me that 'Karma' continues to receive interest and comment from different parts of the world – which, aside from being Arcanum No. 20, is exactly what it was intended to do.

9 Holy Days in Ancient Lands

I had always longed to see the ancient sites and temples of the Goddess in Greece, and, as Ian also thought this was a good idea, we began an orgy of foreign travel.

The sacred site at Delphi was originally dedicated to the Earth Mother, although later Apollo usurped the Mother's position, and a temple was raised in his honour. Among the exhibits in the museum at Delphi was the *omphalos* a strange carved stone of phallic shape once known as the 'navel of the world', which survived the fire at Delphi in 548 BC and the earthquake of 373 BC, during which many of the temple's treasures were lost to the world.

Legend has it that Zeus sent forth two eagles to fly round the world in opposite directions, and their paths intersected over Delphi, which was thereafter interpreted as the earth's sacred centre. The place where the *omphalos* once stood was the point from which the temple was orientated, the four cardinal points marked, and the whole area quartered. The stone itself was the *axis mundi* – the place where the two worlds, material and spiritual, met. It was *between* the worlds, and the gateway into both, in much the same way as the Magic Circle of the witches is recognized as being 'between the worlds'. From here the oracle of Delphi would 'journey' to the inner world and bring back prophecies for the suppliant and for many thousands of souls the oracle's prophecies were borne out to the very letter.

Near its end, Delphi fell under the sway of the Romans, and in the fourth century AD the Emperor Theodosios eliminated the Pythia altogether. The last prophecy from the priestess of the Oracle was given to the Emperor Julian: 'Tell ye the King, the carven hall is fallen in decay; Apollo hath no chapel left, no prophesying bay, no talking spring. The stream is dry that has too much to say.'

The Parthenon in Athens deserved two visits. It is the survivor of many previous temples on the site, all destroyed by various invaders, but a wonderful programme in the Open University television series showed the original façade of this temple of the Goddess. It was coloured in bright blue, red and green with golden pediments, and inside stood a forty-foot-high statue of Athena made of gold and ivory. A pool of water surrounded the statue to keep the ivory from cracking in the heat, and at night the pool reflected the flames from torches, making the Goddess shimmer and appear lifelike. The sculptured frieze high up above the colonnade once contained what are now called the Elgin Marbles, which depicted the story of the birth of the Goddess. Some of these sculptures are now preserved in the British Museum, despite pressure from the government of Greece for their return to Athens.

Nearby, the Erechtheum, probably the oldest cult site on the Acropolis, once housed an ancient wooden statue of the Goddess. This Palladium was considered to be most sacred and to protect the city which owned it. A wooded area near the base of the Acropolis contained a cave-shrine to Pan. Unfortunately, it was fenced off at the time we visited.

Eleusis, the ancient site of the cult of the Mysteries, is not on the tourist map. It covers a large, flat area near the sea north-west of Athens and has its own Acropolis as a backdrop. Half-an-hour's trip on a rattling bus, over more or less the same route as the ancient processional way from Athens, brought us there – curiously, on 23 September, the date when the ancient festival at Eleusis, began.

It was a broiling hot day as we walked over the baking slabs of smooth grey stones. A pillar at the entrance revealed the Goddess, seated, and being handed gifts by a devotee, and other stones in the Lesser Propylaia (or outer court), were beautifully carved with the double poppy and Demeter's sheaves of wheat, which figured prominently in the Eleusinian Mysteries. Most of the excavated artifacts from the site are now in the National Museum in Athens, but certain things remain that help us imaginitively to understand the holiness of Eleusis such as the well where Demeter sat and grieved for her daughter, Persephone, and the cave where Persephone was carried off by Hades to the Underworld. We drank wine; made a libation at the well and absorbed the Spirit of Place. Its ambience was one of peace and sanctity, no doubt preserved by the lack of visitors.

We walked on, past the ruins of small temples, towards the Telesterion – the great Hall of the Mysteries, once barred to non-initiates by huge gates. Deep grooves in the flagstones revealed that the gates opened inwards, and there were also ruts in the stones, made by wagons passing through to the inner sanctum.

The Hall where the Mysteries were revealed in the form of a drama, was surrounded by tiers of stone seats. The initiates who watched these sacred rites were forbidden to divulge what occurred, and the thousands who attended kept the secrets, for nothing has found its way into records. The Hall was rebuilt many times over the centuries, but a smaller building within it, the Anaktoron, always retained its original position. It was inside this walled and windowless structure that the most sacred of the rituals took place, and these rites were only witnessed by those who had been elevated to the second degree of initiation. A probation period of a year and a day was necessary before initiates achieved this higher position and became known as the *epoptae*. They were the ones who were shown 'the holy things' and became familiar with the 'unutterable words'. They, too, were pledged to secrecy, and these vows were faithfully observed during the course of 1700 years.

The level at which the oath was taken must have been most profound. Pindar wrote that 'he who has seen the holy things and goes in death beneath the earth is happy: for he knows life's end and he knows too the new divine beginning.' And Cicero, four hundred years later, remarked that 'the greatest gift of Athens to mankind and the holiest is the Eleusinian Mysteries.'

A coach trip to the Peloponnese disgorged its passengers (including Ian and myself) at Corinth. But Old Corinth, once a classical city of 300,000 souls, is today nothing but a few straggling houses near the ruins of a temple to Apollo (the modern city of New Corinth lies 5½ kilometres away).

St Paul came here and railed against the city's whores, causing a riot and getting himself hounded out of town. He was of course, talking about the Temple of Aphrodite which sat on the summit of the amazing mountain of Acrocorinth and was served by a thousand sacred prostitutes. This mountain rises precipitously 1,885 feet above Corinth and takes about two hours to climb. I wondered why the temple had been placed in such an inaccessible spot, but perhaps there had been method in their madness – having scaled the Acrocorinth, a man would hardly be in a fit state to enjoy the charms of a priestess of Aphrodite!

Our particular tour omitted Olympia, but I thought of the famous Olympic Games which originated there. They began in a foot-race run by girls, to establish which one would become the priestess of the Moon Goddess, Hera. They emerged to begin the race from a tunnel connecting the arena with the Temple of Hera. The event took place in September, or Parthenios (the month 'of the maiden'), but the frequency of the race is not known. Later, another race was introduced for young men, who ran for the privilege of winning the hand of the priestess – a dangerous privilege, for in time the winner would lose his life to his successor.

On the island of Crete we arrived at our hotel at the beginning of a new day. From our balcony, the bay of Agios Nikolaos was quite beautiful, with the mountains dipping into the sea and painted purple in the half-light.

Of the many places we planned to visit, Knossos was high on the list. The customary coach-trip to this site proved to be unavoidable, but we refrained from joining the clusters of tourists who hung on each word spoken by their guides as though it was a divine revelation. There is something about the jargon they trip out so repetitively that makes me want to shake their air of smug authority by challenging them on some point, and risk being answered by a basilisk stare of disbelief that one of their 'sheep' had dared to contradict them. (I do realize, however, that if it were not for the guides many people would leave a site as unenlightened as when they arrived.) So, armed with a map of the Palace and our

163

previously acquired knowledge of these ruins, we set out to explore for ourselves.

Descending a wide staircase into the gloomy depths of what was once a building at least four storeys high, we arrived at the first lower level, where among other dark rooms the 'Queen's Bedroom' is situated. This was the name given to it by the British anthropologist and archaeologist Sir Arthur Evans, who excavated Knossos in 1900. Out of a palace of around twelve hundred interconnected rooms, stairways, cellars and corridors, this small, damp and airless room was the only one that Evans deemed appropriate for a queen!

Evans began excavating a Bronze Age site near the city of Herakleion and came across a huge building. Immediately, he associated it with the legendary King Minos and announced that here was the palace of the ancient king and his queen. Evans also coined the name 'Minoan' for the people who lived in Bronze Age Crete, although even today no one knows what they were really called. (Ancient Egyptian wall-paintings in Third Dynasty tombs reveal typical Cretan processions, with people carrying objects identical to those found in Crete, and these people are clearly labelled, 'Keftiu', or people of the islands. Cretans?) We are however, indebted to Sir Arthur Evans for his work and the time and money he ploughed into these excavations. The people of Crete also have much to thank him for in terms of revenue, and on entering Knossos the visitor will see a bronze bust of the man whose discovery brought him and Crete, immortality.

One strange anomaly at Knossos is the 'Queen's Bathtub'. This, too, lies in the dark, subterranean levels, and it is quite small, with a drainage hole but no provision for waste water in the floor. Stranger still, is the 'Queen's Toilet' – a niche in the wall, at the bottom of which a drainage channel vanishes into the floor. Was this really a *flush* toilet, the acme of a civilized nation and perfected by the Cretans more than thirty-five hundred years ago?

We stepped out into a small room where the queen would sit with her women, apparently working on handicrafts. (Down here – in the dark?) A narrow rectangle in the ceiling showed the deep blue sky far above, but the walls of the shaft once rose four storeys high. Was it really here, in the bowels of the earth, the queen chose to live? It was extraordinary, and also rather creepy. I was glad to move on.

Entering the 'Throne Room' on an upper storey, I started to feel decidedly uneasy. The room was semi-lit from doorways and a light shaft, and the throne was set in the centre of a long wall decorated with paintings of kneeling griffins and strange plants. The atmosphere was oppressive, and everyone who came into this room was soon subdued and spoke in whispers. When we emerged into the sunlight I recalled something I had read about this 'Throne Room'. The writer said that when the room was discovered, it was decorated with a *river* scene, but this was replaced by the present murals – a fantasy of Evans's painted for effect in 1930. It was all very mysterious, and I could not imagine anyone wanting to live in such a building with so little light and air.

Wandering round the museum in Herakleion we came across a room full of bathtubs. At least that was what the one at Knossos had been called – but here they were labelled sarcophagi. I tried to ask an official why the one at Knossos was called the 'Queen's Bathtub', but he merely smiled and shrugged. Stupid of me to ask, I suppose!

A few years later on the island of Rhodes, I came across an opinion of Knossos that was very different from that of Evans. I spotted a small but very well-stocked bookshop in Rhodes Town and dived in to browse. One book that immediately caught my eye was called *The Secret of Crete* by Hans Georg Wunderlich. The author, a geologist, had written of his own personal examination of Knossos and concluded that the so-called 'Palace of King Minos', was nothing more or less than a vast mortuary temple; a City of the Dead. It served not only for the preparation of the corpse before burial but for the entire panoply of services required – from stonemasons and embalmers right through to the religious rituals and dramas enacted for both the departed, and the mourners. Reading that the 'Queen's Bathtub' was one of the many sarcophagi discovered at Knossos, and similar to those in the Herakleion museum, I knew that my feelings about the 'palace' had been correct.

There was also the common use, for burial purposes, of

pithoi, the large, ornamental jars found in their hundreds at the site. These differ from oil containers, being shoulder-wide at the neck. Oil jars have plain surfaces and are deliberately narrow at the mouth, therefore much easier to seal. The manner of burial obviously depended upon what the dead person's relatives could afford. Embalming (several methods used), burial in *pithoi* or sarcophagi, and cremation, according to the beautiful cinerary urn, decorated with a statue of the Goddess, which was found at Knossos. Moreover, in connection with the 'Throne of Minos', Wunderlich discusses Etruscan tombs, where as many as five such chairs (thrones) were situated next to the burial vaults. It would seem that no living person, king or commoner, sat on *that* 'throne'. The dead were venerated during the period of mourning – the period it took to dry out an embalmed corpse – and during that time they were seated on special chairs with high backs and a seat that was either hollowed out or had a ridge at the front to prevent the corpse from sliding off – just like the 'throne' at Knossos. Again as echoed at Knossos, many of these chairs had three indentations at each side, for belts to support the corpse, whose eyes, according to custom, were open, and seemingly staring into infinity. No wonder the atmosphere in the 'Throne Room' had been oppressive and enough to make visitors speak in lowered voices!

I cannot possibly convey the depths this book touches. Wunderlich's knowledge of the customs of Ancient Egypt and adjacent cultures, combined with his technical expertise, is brought to bear in his detective work at Knossos. For anyone interested, *The Secret of Crete* is published by P. Efstathiadis Group, 14, Valtetsiou Street, Athens.

Another 'must' for us was the Diktaion Cave, high up in the mountains of Crete, and long associated in legend with the birthplace of Zeus, who was hidden there from the machinations of his murderous father, Chronos, the Father of the Gods.

Zeus was born of the Great Goddess, Rhea, who gave birth to the Divine Child in Crete and thus established the original concept of such worship. According to Robert Graves, Zeus was annually reborn in Rhea's cave at midwinter, when the

166

sun entered the sign of Capricornus, as were other sun-gods such as Apollo and Mithras.

There is a steep climb to the cave from the point where the coach disgorges its passengers, and men with donkeys offer their animals to take you to the top of the mountain. (We declined, not wishing our weight on their backs to cause yet another difficult journey for the poor beasts that travel up and down that mountain all day to earn their masters' bread.) A plateau at the top reveals the huge, dark entrance to the cave, with groups of people continuously either emerging or descending into the heart of the mountain.

We were given small, lighted candles and walked down a steep path covered with loose stones. There was nothing to hang on to – no rail or rope to steady oneself – and the pitiful flame of the candle was devoured by the Stygian darkness. At the bottom, we were shown the stalagmites and stalactites, in what seemed to be an enclosed area to the left of the cave. The guide lifted his lamp to point out what looked like a baby's face and body on the wall. This, he declared, was the new-born Zeus! Strangely , the stalactites and stalagmites *have* formed the features of a very young child, and this natural phenomenon has occurred at the site of the legend and in perfect harmony with it.

After passing through the uppper hall, where many bronze objects were found, including knives, bracelets and small replicas of the Labrys (the Minoan double-headed axe), we descended further into the abyss. Here an explorer once placed his candle in a cleft, where the flame revealed a bronze knife wedged upright between the stalagmites. Of Mycenaean origin, it was far older than anything discovered in the sacred enclosure above. Many hundreds of offerings have been chiselled out of the stalactites and stalagmites that had gradually covered them over a period of at least four thousand years. Originally, they would have been placed in the niches between the candle-like deposits, then drop by drop, the water dripped down until they were enclosed in transparent shrouds.

Down there, in the darkness, I thought of the people who had left these personal offerings to their god so long ago. Had *they* also stumbled over stones as they approached the sacred depths? I imagined them holding their flaming torches on high to keep the blackness at bay, then carefully depositing their gifts with a prayer for the god to look kindly upon them. In their time they would have had no fear of their offerings being stolen from the Cave of Zeus. No one would dare to steal from the god himself, and their precious objects remained a testimony to that trust over long eons of time.

One evening, Ian and I went for a leisurely stroll and came to a lane on the outskirts of Agios Nikolaos. The sun was nearing the horizon, and the air was pleasantly cool. We passed some bungalows, where an alsatian barked a warning, and came to a low white-washed wall which bounded a cemetery, where tiny coloured lights glowed and the bent backs of two black-robed women could be seen, tending the graves. All the graves had pictures of the deceased on the headstones and most of the epitaphs revealed that they had died, young, in road accidents. It was slightly disconcerting to see the smiling likenesses of those buried there, illuminated by the lamps amidst those sombre surroundings.

As soon as we stepped inside the gates of the graveyard, we experienced a sudden change in the atmosphere. The place was vibrating with a numinous intensity. My skin crawled with the familiar tingling sensation, as I realized that these were etheric vibrations – and strong ones, too. The entire graveyard was pulsating with these emanations and the happy faces of the departed seemed uncannily alive, as if at any moment they might suddenly appear from the shadows. We felt as though we were on the threshold of the Unseen World. It was unsettling.

The women had disappeared, the sun had set, and in the twilight the grave lights were brighter than ever: scattered stars of blue, red, gold, green and purple – a rainbow of remembrance. As we walked back to the hotel, we discussed the phenomenon. Had it anything to do with the climate? Could a dry, warm climate nourish and sustain the etheric body longer than a cold, wet one? Ian suggested that it could have something to do with the relatives and friends of the dead lighting candles and gazing at the photographs of their loved ones. Were they holding on to the dead by these vigils, and so keeping them close to the Earth Plane?

In the Western Mysteries, we are taught to refrain from yearning for those who have passed on, as this inhibits the soul's passage in the other world. Too many tears, too much sorrow, disturbs these travellers in a new land and impedes their progress in the spiritual realms. Despite our deep sorrow and anguish when a loved one goes ahead, the best thing is to send our love to them and wish them well upon their journey.

Hot countries do not appear to have ghosts, yet the Western World, with its damp and misty environment, would seem to be a haven for them. Is it easier, therefore, for a soul in its astral body, to manifest in the material world if the climate is suitable? Remembering that the Astral Plane is composed of the ethereal qualities of Water, such may be the case.

When the Earth had travelled once more around the Sun, we were on our way to Malta, and looking forward to seeing the many temples of the Goddess excavated there. I carried with me a very good article on the island by Chris Bray, which explained some unique aspects of these temples and made me all the more eager to visit them. Malta also held links with Arnold, as he spent some time there during World War II, entertaining the troops while the island was under attack. (For the record, Arnold performed his act 4,000 feet up in the air, in a DC-3 transport aircraft en route from Tripoli to Malta, on 10 November 1943.) Some forty years later Ian and I arrived at Luqa airport during a strike by the airport staff. We had to sit in the plane for an hour, which proved to be the least comfortable part of our journey.

Another slight hitch occurred when we reached the hotel. The bedroom had no sea view – in fact, no view at all. The solitary window looked onto an internal shaft in the centre of the hotel, with aromas from the kitchen wafting up it and into our room. We tackled the manager immediately, and the next day moved into a lovely airy room overlooking the bay. The manager had been married in Sheffield; perhaps that was one reason for our swift transfer.

Some of the temple sites were in isolated parts of the island, so we hired a car. We were warned that to the Maltese the most important consideration was always to drive in the shade. The *Maltese Calypso* has a relevant verse:

> The one thing that made me very cross,
> Everyone drives like Stirling Moss,
> And the motor cars here are a bit of a joke,
> Old and green and make lots of smoke.
> The smallest book in the world I'm told
> That's the Maltese Highway Code!

One bonus was the fact that they drive on the left, so we hired a Ford Fiesta with only 4,000 miles on the clock, and really enjoyed driving through the countryside.

The Copper Age remains of Hagar Qim, and nearby Mnajdra, lie on the west coast of Malta. Before the excavations in 1839 all that could be seen of them was a mound of earth from which the tops of the huge stones peeped out. There is plenty to see now as you wander round the ruins: passages, an oracular room and huge dressed stones, which make you realize what magnificent places these temples once were.

Many headless statues of the Goddess were found at Hagar Qim; some seated, others standing. The heads were lying on the ground, but they were far from being vandalized. Examination of the figures revealed sockets between the shoulders, to receive the heads, and there were various heads wearing different expressions, so they were obviously changed from time to time – perhaps to coincide with a particular season of the year. One extremely interesting aspect of the temples has to do with their *shape*. They were built in the actual form of a female, and as those people visualized the Goddess i.e. as an obese, pregnant woman. This shape is clearly visible in the maps and drawings of these temples, and is universally acknowledged.

We had arrived in Malta on the twenty-fifth anniversary of the island's independence, and Valletta was celebrating in a big way. The streets were ablaze with pink and orange bunting and the red and white of the Maltese flag. Colour and excitement were everywhere. Without realizing its significance I happened to be wearing red and white that day – an appropriate coincidence!

170

Arnold once mentioned a street in Valletta known to sailors as 'The Gut'. Where ladies of the world's oldest profession would lean out of their windows and chat to each other across the long, but extremely narrow street. I had to find it, and heard that it was now called 'Straight Street'! Had the ladies also gone on the 'straight and narrow'? We located the thoroughfare and put it on film.

Above Mellieha Bay is the town of that name, sitting on its commanding ridge and looking across the sea towards Gozo. Below stretches the most beautiful beach in Malta, studded with blue and white awnings and sun-worshippers in various stages of sun-burn, such as nearly-done, well-done, and, 'Have I caught the sun, or what!' I had read somewhere of an ancient cave at Mellieha where prehistoric man worshipped the Goddess, but no one seemed to know where it was. We asked around, until someone said, 'Do you mean the Grotto?' We thought it best to say, 'Yes', and were told to cross the road, and go down the steps and we would find it. The steps led to another flight which changed direction, and there, in the side of the cliff and beneath the road, a dark opening led to more steps descending into a cave.

From the entrance we could see lots of coloured lights and benches placed in rows, and as we walked down there were pieces of clothing and other items hanging on the walls. The cave had become a grotto to the Virgin and Child: a shrine of healing. At the back, on a plinth set in a pool of water, a white marble statue of Mary, with the infant Jesus sitting upon her shoulder, held out a hand in welcome. In front of the pool an altar, also of white marble, held fresh flowers, letters and more lighted candles.

We sat for a while, meditating on the aeons during which this cave had been regarded as a sacred place. It had a remarkable and benevolent atmosphere, and there was also a feeling that it was protected and cherished. The letters and photographs were requests for healing, and the framed pictures celebrated a loved one's return to health.

Issuing from a dark opening, the Sacred Spring – the Blood of the Earth – was the focus of this cave. The Goddess and the Sacred Spring have always been One; the Waters of Life, Birth and Death (the Astral Plane), are part of her living body.

171

Moreover, to early man and woman, there would be no dichotomy in using the cave both as a home and a place of worship. In those far-off days, gods and men lived very closely together. We were glad to have persevered in our search for this place.

The jewel in the crown of Maltese temples, is the Hal Saflieni Hypogeum in Paola, a suburb of Valletta. This temple lies deep underground and was discovered by accident in 1902 when workmen were digging drains. Today it is approached through an entrance hall, where after purchasing your ticket, you pass through to the yard at the rear. A modern spiral staircase then leads you down forty feet beneath the surface and into prehistoric times. There are three levels of buildings covering an area of 8,600 square feet. Today they are illuminated by electricity, but five thousand years ago, man created this fascinating temple in the darkness, with only flaring brands at his disposal.

Part of the temple looks like a subterranean Stonehenge, especially in what is now called the Holy of Holies, with its curved-in walls, niches, doorways, and corbelling. It also resembles some of the ground-level temples on Malta. As you walk round the many rooms, negotiating the steps that lead from one level to another, you marvel at this immense structure. Here, was found a statue of the Goddess, again with two heads by its side, and the famous 'sleeping lady' terracotta of an obese woman lying on a boat-shaped trestle bed. She wears a long, frilled skirt, and *appears* to be asleep.

A room called the Oracle Chamber has a niche quite large enough for a person to crawl into, and one could well imagine a priestess/prophetess of the Goddess lying in her 'Moon-boat' inside this hollow, in a trance-sleep, receiving communications from the Ancestors.

The Oracle Chamber is supposed to resound with a peculiar echo, but only in response to a male voice. I therefore decided to put this to the test, and at an appropriate moment I intoned certain vowel sounds, slowly and deliberately. Not only did they resonate throughout the entire complex, their echoes were heard high above in the entrance hall (much to the discomfort of the attendants, one of whom rushed down, immediately). The effect of the sonics quite stupefied me,

172

too. It was as though a great bell had been struck, its thunderous reverberations repeatedly crashing on the eardrums. Most of the tourists (none apparently English) were now eagerly crowding round the entrance to this chamber, and Ian suddenly became engrossed with his shoelaces. (Poor love, at the best of times he dislikes being in the limelight – especially for the wrong reasons.)

The attendant was waving his arms about and remonstrating in broken English, but I was not in the least perturbed. I merely looked down at him, as from a great height (not difficult, given his stature) and loudly announced that I had debunked, once and for all, the belief that the echo effect could only be achieved by a male voice. Then I stalked out of the room through the milling throng of visitors. Of course, I had put on a bit of an act, just for the fun of it, but what was so terrible about intoning a few sounds? I hadn't torn the place apart with my bare hands.

Ian was talking to the attendant (he is very good at pouring oil on troubled waters), and eventually, the guide approached me and said, apologetically, that if I had told them of my deep interest in temples such as this one, they would have allowed me to explore it privately. (They probably thought that this would have saved other visitors from being deafened by my vocalisations!) I *do* realize that people are entitled to see these sites, but I feel frustrated when so many walk round in ignorance of the deity for whom the temples were erected. As it was, after the visitors had gone we were allowed some extra time, for which we were duly grateful.

As Malta is an island with very little rainfall it has been suggested that the most important request asked of the Goddess was for a good, hefty downpour. No doubt the priestesses of the temples performed many rituals to this end. Be that as it may, a curious thing occurred when we had left the Hypogeum and were having coffee in a nearby bar. Dark clouds appeared quite suddenly in what had previously been a clear blue sky, and a rush of cool air swirled through the streets chasing odd bits of litter in a crazy dance. Lightning streaked across the sky then spoke with an ominous roar, and pedestrians ran for cover to avoid the heavy rainstorm. Ian and I exchanged meaningful glances as we drank our coffee.

173

On Malta's tiny sister island of Gozo we saw a sign which read, 'The Gozo Heritage – the Living Experience!' Intrigued, we passed through a garden, bought tickets and walked into a large convenience store! A young lady approached, took our tickets and opened a door to the left of the entrance. We stepped inside, the door closed behind us, and we were alone and in utter darkness.

Very soon, there was a slow building of blood-red light, and in that light we were confronted by an immense replica of the goddess statue from the Tarxien temple, with its pleated skirt and the tiny feet. Here, though there was a passageway between the legs. Models of worshippers knelt in front of the image, all bathed in the crimson light. It was extremely effective.

Then, the commentary began: 'I AM THE GODDESS!' The voice was strong yet melodious, and so moving that my skin prickled and my face crawled with goose-bumps. It was completely unexpected to see the Goddess portrayed realistically for a change. We stood there, enthralled, while she spoke of many things and of how she was 'mother' to the Earth and all that lived upon it. The narration over, the light died, and the passageway became illuminated. We passed under the great statue and into another time capsule.

There were many rooms, each depicting a different part of the island's history, until we came face to face with the Union Jack in a framework that encompassed Britain's involvement with the Maltese islands. So at the end of this 'living experience', the Union Jack, incorporating the red, white and blue colours of the Goddess Triformis (Mother, Virgin and Crone), continues to express, albeit unknowingly, the numinous presence of the Great Goddess and consolidates the friendship between these two nations.

Seemingly insatiable for foreign travel, our next visit was to Rhodes. This is another island that acknowledges the triple aspect of the Goddess. According to Robert Graves, Rhodes belonged to the Sumerian Moon-Goddess, Dam-Kina-Danae, and three of its major cities were named Cameira, Ialysa, and Linda (Lindos), indicative of the Threefold One.

Mandraki harbour is graced by the statues of a stag and a doe which stand on pillars looking out to sea. Their presence is due to the Delphic Oracle. The story goes that at one time in its history Rhodes was overrun by snakes, and the oracle advised the people to bring deer to the island and they would have no more trouble. Apparently, snakes cannot endure the smell of deer, and the plan was successful. Deer now run wild in the mountains and have become a symbol of Rhodes into the bargain. But I wonder what happened to the snakes? Did they disappear beneath the ground never to be seen again, or did they pack their snakeskin bags and take the first ship to leave the harbour? In my mind's eye I could see queues of these creatures on the harbour walls and slithering aboard craft bound for more hospitable climes.

The Archaeological Museum in Rhodes Old Town holds the famous marble statue of Aphrodite Thalassia, from the 3rd century BC. One day in 1929 it got tangled in a fisherman's net and was drawn from its resting-place at the bottom of the sea. Lawrence Durrell gives a most telling description of the statue in his *Reflections on a Marine Venus*:

> The seawater had sucked at her for centuries till she was like some white stone jujube, with hardly a feature sharp as the burin must originally have left it. Yet such was the grace of her composition – the slender neck and breasts on that richly modelled torso, the supple line of arm and thigh – that the absence of firm outline only lent her a soft and confusing grace. Instead of sharp Classical features she had been given something infinitely more adolescent, unformed. The ripeness of her body was offset by the face, not of a Greek matron, but of a young girl.

The statue has a round copper-coloured mark on the right breast where a metal object – a coin(?) had lain while it rested beneath the waves.

Another statue in this museum is often referred to as the Aphrodite of Rhodes. It was unearthed in Rhodes Town in 1912 and is dated to the first century BC. This Aphrodite is kneeling and holding out her long curling hair to dry in the sun. Her naked body is of perfect proportions with softly-rounded limbs, and is much more life-like than some portrayals of the Love Goddess.

175

When we went to Cyprus we found the 'Baths of Aphrodite', where the Goddess is said to have bathed. Surrounded by overhanging foliage, the dark pool looked uninviting. However, local legend says that to bathe in it brings an especial beauty to one's features seven hours later, so many people had come prepared for a dip. Ignoring the greenish slime that invades a pool hidden from sunlight, they splashed merrily about while onlookers made unkind remarks to the effect that certain bathers would need more than one immersion to effect a transformation. Everyone was highly amused until a water-snake was seen, gliding sinuously between the stones. It was most probably a harmless reptile, but it emptied the pool in a flash! (I bathed my face and paddled in a small overflow, but as far as I could tell there was no obvious improvement to my features. My feet, however, are now much prettier – well, that's *my* story and I'm sticking to it!)

On the two-hour journey to the capital, Nicosia, I thought of Gerald Gardner. He had been no stranger to Cyprus and had even purchased land on the island. The National Museum to which we were heading was where Gerald had shown the then curator how the ancient Cypriots hafted their swords. And after lunch in a nice restaurant opposite the museum, we retraced Gerald's steps.

It was a fine museum with many artefacts and statues, some dated tentatively to 4,000 BC, but likely to be far older. Strange, primitive images of the Goddess with the barest hint of facial features had a dignity, a curious majesty, about them, even when standing in glass cases. Banal inscriptions, such as 'figures of unknown origin', or 'nymph', accompanied most of them, but more recent ones were given the name 'goddess'. All the same, walking round the rooms you realize the immensity of what was once the 'Religion of the Goddess' and remember that, in Cyprus and other countries, figurines such as these are merely the remnants that escaped attention during the destruction of the world's oldest faith.

According to the museum authorities, one of the most beautiful exhibits was a 'statue of a horned god' from the Sanctuary of the Horned God at Enkomi. This statue was wearing a helmet with the horns attached to it, like those worn by priests of the Old Religion. It is therefore much more likely to be a representation of a *priest* of the Horned God. On a statue of the god himself, the horns would issue from the *head*, as with other horned deities, notably Pan.

When flying to these distant lands I have never lost my sense of wonder at being transported through the air to my destination in the space of a few hours. I still consider it to be amazing – a miracle of man's inventiveness. Likewise, being able to converse with a friend, thousands of miles away, by merely lifting a telephone receiver, is to me, astonishing. Yet, in this blasé, 'take-everything-for-granted' society of ours, it may not be a bad thing to own up to a little naiveté.

10   Witches of the New World

In 1989 Eileen Smith, a High Priestess of the Craft from Florida, came to visit me. I found her a very friendly, happy person who was dedicated to the Craft of the Wise and had a long association with it. After that first meeting we kept in touch, and one day Eileen rang to say it would be an excellent idea if Ian and I could come over one Hallowe'en and attend South Florida's Samhain Ball, an event which Eileen had organized for many years. I was also booked to give a lecture – an excellent opportunity to meet witches and occultists from different parts of the States. So it was, that in October 1992 we were airborne and looking forward to linking up with 'Children of the Goddess' in the New World. We were not disappointed. On that initial visit, a transatlantic bond was forged that I hope will never be broken – a special bond of affection and goodfellowship.

It was good to see Eileen again, and we were soon chattering away over a meal. Someone said I really 'gelled' with them, and I wondered if it had anything to do with the fact that the USA is considered by astrologers to be ruled by the sign of Gemini, a sign that is heavily emphasized in my natal chart. Whatever the reason, I felt a strong affinity, an instant attraction.

One evening we had a special invitation to dine at the Miami home of Robin and Dwina Gibb. Robin is part of the world-famous trio the Bee-Gees, and his wife is an author of some repute as well as being patroness of the British order of 'Bards, Ovates and Druids', the first female recipient of this honour in three hundred years. Eileen, a friend of Dwina's, had mentioned we were coming over, and this had resulted in the kind invitation (apparently, Dwina had known of me for a long time and was keen to meet me personally).

The gates swung open at our approach, and Dwina greeted us at the door of her Florida home, a large, white elegant mansion overlooking the sea. I took to her right away; she was so friendly and lovely to look at, as well as being a gracious hostess. We were ushered into her study – a book-lined room, and introduced to Donna, her private secretary, who was a jolly, bespectacled lady.

Dinner, a vegetarian meal interspersed with animated conversation, was eaten in a spacious dining-room, and we sat at one end of a table large enough to accommodate twenty people. Afterwards, in a comfy lounge, Dwina showed me a fascinating way to read the Tarot cards. Then Robin came in, having returned from a recording session at his studios. It was really great to meet him in the flesh.

Before we left, Dwina presented me with an autographed copy of her book *Cormac – the Seers*, the first volume of a trilogy. When I read it, I realized what a great gift Dwina had for describing Ireland's Celtic past. Her writing captures the poetry and magic of that ancient kingdom. Being Irish by birth, she has an incredible knowledge and insight into things Celtic and an innate sense of the spiritual beliefs of her native land.

The following night, I again met Dwina, but this time it was upon the Astral Plane. I wondered about this, because for it to be a genuine out-of-the-body experience, Dwina must also have been aware of it. There were other people present when I next saw Dwina, and the incident had temporarily slipped from my mind until she suddenly exclaimed, 'That was an amazing encounter the other night, Patricia!' Her words proved the veracity of the experience in no uncertain terms.

Dwina drove us deep into the Everglades to meet a very special American Indian. She had come to know Rony Jimmy and his wife Mary Jimmy after a terrible hurricane struck that area, when she had organized aid and supplies for the Indians to repair damage done to their homes and crops. Our party also included Eileen and Donna, and we eventually arrived at a cluster of small shops and dwellings. Under an awning a table covered with a snow-white cloth was laid for lunch. Rony Jimmy and his wife were charming people, smiling and welcoming us to their land. With cool drinks to hand, we sat in the shade and listened with intense interest as Rony expounded the religious beliefs of his tribe.

Soon after sitting down, and despite the heat of the day, my skin began to crawl with the tingling sensation that for me always denotes a spiritual presence. It was so strong it quite took my breath away, as the numinous energy weaved around me. Rony noticed my reaction, and laughed, 'It is only the ancestors. They have come to have a look at you.' He spoke as though it was an everyday occurrence. I laughed too, 'How wonderful! We are extremely privileged.' He nodded. 'You could say that. They do not come for everyone.' Mentally, I thanked the Great Spirits for their interest, and hoped they approved of us.

Rony Jimmy's concepts of the after-life were not too dissimilar from those of the Old Religion, but there was one important exception. The American Indians do not believe in reincarnation. They affirm that the soul enters an inner world to dwell for all time with the ancestors of the tribes.

After an excellent lunch which included mouth-watering sweet pancakes made by Mary Jimmy from a secret recipe, we reluctantly took our leave. To have established a personal link with these people who belonged to the Miccosukee Tribe of South Florida, was indeed gratifying.

Around one hundred people were expected for my lecture. Almost as soon as we arrived, people came up with all manner of gifts – a red rose, a goddess brooch, a ring – it was so unexpected! One of the most unusual, from a High Priest in Massachusetts, was the badge of the Salem Police – a witch flying on her broomstick, a waning moon and the words, 'The Witch City, Massachusetts, 1626' (this was the date of the Salem witch trials). Another amazing present was a marvellous pair of statues representing the God and the Goddess, wrought from a special material used in space-flights. (As it happened, I had prepared around sixty small gifts to pass round as keepsakes, so I was able to give as well as receive.)

Before the talk, Eileen introduced everyone present – or

rather she indicated each person, who then volunteered their name and position in the Craft, the name of their coven (if they had one) and where it was situated. By the time she introduced me I had already spied a video camera on a tripod, aimed in my direction (Eileen later informed me that the video of my talk was rapidly being worn out because so many witches wanted to view it). At the end, I received a generous ovation, and Eileen whispered, 'You were magnificent.' Praise, indeed!

Knowing how close I had been to Gerald Gardner, Eileen had hinted that the audience would love to hear more about the man himself in his everyday life. I therefore included in my talk some amusing incidents that occurred while I was in Gerald's company, and, judging from the mirth they evoked, I think they were appeciated. I also delivered a special message from Gerald Gardner himself. And in order to explain this mystery, it is necessary to digress. Two weeks earlier I had been performing a scrying operation, using a rather special obsidian sphere which I find indispensable for divination of this kind.

When I thought that particular procedure was over, I sensed Gerald Gardner's presence very strongly, and then, clairaudiently, heard his voice. He seemed quite agitated: 'Pat! I say Pat! You must tell them in America that Louis Wilkinson was a member of the New Forest coven at the time I was initiated into it.' He went on to say that Wilkinson had refuted this for several reasons, and that it was quite all right to mislead people in those days (the late 1930s), because the Craft and those within it had to be protected. The witches were afraid some sort of persecution would be revived if it came to the ears of the Establishment.

I understood what Gerald was on about. Dr Louis Umfraville Wilkinson (Louis Marlow, the writer) had been a close friend of Aleister Crowley from their Cambridge days and had performed Crowley's *Gnostic Requiem* at the latter's funeral in Brighton crematorium on 5 December 1947. (This included the famous *Hymn to Pan* and other excerpts from *Liber Legis* and *Magick*.) Crowley had described Wilkinson as a world-famous Shakespearean lecturer and scholar.

Gerald's message was interesting. In his book *Ritual Magic in England* Francis King mentions how in 1953 he met Wilkinson, who was then living in the Dorset village of Hazelbury Bryan. They discussed Crowley, and Wilkinson said that his friend had been offered initiation into the Craft of the Witches as a young man, but had turned down the offer because 'he didn't want to be bossed around by women'. (This statement of Crowley's has appeared in print many times, but it is relevant to the context of this account.) When King pooh-poohed the story, Wilkinson defended Crowley, saying that he believed his friend had been telling the truth, because he, Wilkinson, had known several members of a New Forest coven in the late 1930s or early 1940s. Another source quotes Wilkinson as saying that he himself could have joined this coven, had he so wished. And now here was Gerald (albeit a discarnate Gerald) declaring that Wilkinson had indeed been a member of that coven!

In my own experience, spirit messages have regularly proved to be accurate, and so I see no reason to doubt Gerald's sudden and unexpected intrusion upon my thoughts. All the more so, since he was talking about someone I had never known, and whose name was the last thing on my mind at that particular moment. As I mulled over Gerald's words, it seemed to me that what he had said was the truth of the matter, i.e. that Wilkinson had indeed been an initiate of that coven. Otherwise, why would Gerald have contacted me, and been so anxious for me to inform the witches in the States about it?

A book of Wilkinson's memoirs, *Seven Friends*, with an introduction by his son Oliver Wilkinson, was recently published by Mandrake Press in 1992, and apparently nowhere in this volume is witchcraft even mentioned. As the title suggests, the book is devoted to Wilkinson's friendships with several famous people, including Oscar Wilde, Somerset Maugham and, of course, Aleister Crowley.

It is said that upon the Inner Planes time, as we know it, does not exist, and events in the material world are observed as something like an eternal Now. The question is, did Gerald know that *Seven Friends* was being prepared when he came through to me, and/or did he consider that it was high time for the truth about Wilkinson's apparent affiliation to the

New Forest coven to be revealed? Mysteries such as this one have a peculiar habit of exposing themselves, piece by piece, over a period of time, so that eventually, all the strands can be brought together.

Another strange twist of fate involving Gardner and the New Forest coven occurred soon afterwards. Keith Morgan, the editor of *The Deosil Dance*, a popular occult periodical, asked me to write a foreword for a reprint of Gerald Gardner's *High Magic's Aid* that he was publishing. Whilst engaged upon this task, I naturally included the story of the book's difficult birth.

When Gerald had spoken of writing a book on witchcraft (to explain its true meaning), his High Priestess, Dorothy Clutterbuck, was not amused, and told him so in no uncertain terms. It was quite out of the question; it would only bring trouble, and a renewal of the persecutions in some form. No one had ever dared to mention that the Craft of the Wise was still in existence, and it was best for people to think it had died out.

Gerald, however, was not so sure, and he stuck to his guns, taking every opportunity that presented itself to change Dorothy's mind. The Craft needed new blood; the Old Gods required recognition in order to grow strong again; it was time for the return of the Goddess, etc. The answer was still 'No', and it was many years before she relented – and even then a condition was attached. In his biography, *Gerald Gardner – Witch*, Jack Bracelin confirms: 'It was to be another seven years, however, before his fellow-witches would allow him to reveal any of their ideas – even their very existence to the world at large.' (He is referring to the period from 1939 – when Gerald was initiated to 1946, when the necessary permission was finally granted.) The conditions upon which the permission was finally granted were that any information about the Craft and its practices must take the form of fiction. Thus the novel *High Magic's Aid* was finally written, and was published in 1949.

Gerald's behaviour in this dilemma says a lot for his integrity, because, apart from Dorothy's prolonged objections, there was nothing to prevent him from writing a book about witchcraft.

At the time I was writing the foreword to Morgan's reprint, a hand-written letter from Gerald Gardner came to light in America. In it, he tells the recipient about the trouble he had before his novel was written:

. . . Actually, I wanted to write about a witch and what she'd told me, and she wouldn't let me tell anything about witchcraft, but I said why not let me write from the witches' point of view. You are always persecuted and abused. So, she said, I might if I didn't give any Witch magic, and it must only be as fiction. So as I had to give some magic, I simply copied it from the Jewish Ritual Magic, chiefly, 'The Key of Solomon the King'. It was thought that King Solomon could command the spirits and make them work for him. And if you knew these words and sigils you could do the same. This key is usually in Latin or Hebrew, but there is an English translation by MacGregor Mathers. But personally I don't believe that it works. It's all very difficult and complicated . . . .

It is not uncommon for letters from the past to come to light from time to time. However, for a letter written by Gerald Gardner to be resurrected at the time I was writing that foreword, and for it to discuss the very thing I was writing about, seemed to be something more than a coincidence. I would attribute it to the mysterious Finger of Fate, which often confounds time in the most extraordinary ways. Anyway as it was undoubtedly meant to form part of the foreword, it was duly included.

To return to Florida. Questions from the floor followed my talk. One of the most pertinent was 'Can a *man* erect the Circle?' I knew that my reply was awaited with intense curiosity, as apparently there is a strict rule in most American covens that only a woman can perform this function. I agreed with this, but there was one important exception.

If a High Priest wishes to form a coven, hiving off from his parent coven, he must first initiate a female with whom to work. But if he has no such partner, he must ask the Goddess for a suitable person to appear in his life, and work to that end. This obligatory condition fulfilled, he must then train the lady, and in due course initiate her into the Craft. Here, there may be two alternatives. Either the initiation can be performed in the Circle of his parent coven, with his teachers present, or it can be done by erecting the Circle himself. (This latter option was employed by Gerald Gardner when he initiated me.) Thereafter, the new initiate will perform the function of erecting the Circle with her athame on *every* occasion. And when this lady has achieved the Second Degree, she will automatically be entitled to use the Magical Sword. As I said at the time, these were the ways in which *I* was taught.

At the end of this somewhat lengthy, but entirely necessary answer, the room erupted in jubilant cheers, not least, masculine ones. A book-signing session followed, when it was possible to chat to people on a one-to-one basis, and so the evening came to a close.

The Samhain Ball, held in a spacious hall hired for the purpose, was a tribute to Eileen Smith and all the hard work she puts into these celebrations. Fancy Dress is always stipulated, a different theme each year. On this occasion everyone had to be dressed as an Elemental, and the room was full of Dryads, Gnomes, Sylphs and Salamanders in wonderful, glittering costumes. Banners hung at the Four Quarters symbolizing the Four Elements, and in the centre of the dance floor, a small altar held pride of place.

That night, the ritual performed was to improve the fate of monkeys, taken from the wild and transported in tiny crates, without food or water, to laboratories in England and elsewhere for the purposes of vivisection. Many covens in Britain, including my own, had worked magic on the various aspects of cruelty to animals for a long time, and had achieved some success. In the case of Shamrock Farms, one of the receiving centres for the monkeys, an investigation by government officials followed, and a particularly callous and cruel man, who was supposedly looking after the animals, was relieved of his duties. An undercover agent from an Animal Rights group, who infiltrated the place as a worker, filmed the entire disgusting proceedings, a film which was shown on national television.

In the late eighties, and a few weeks after our initial workings, a programme was shown on British television revealing instances of cruelty to animals in some of its multitudinous forms. Since that time, more programmes have been devoted to these shameful practices and continue to be featured.

Eileen opened the ritual, then passed Gerald's sword to me. Twenty-nine years had elapsed since I last wielded it in a magical ceremony. During the rite, people dressed as animals and birds came up to me, one by one. Each related the sad story of man's cruelty to their particular species, and each one was given the Pentacle to hold – a symbol of the Earth and what should be their innate right to dwell upon it in peace and freedom. I placed the Cup, a symbol of the Goddess and Her compassion, upon the Pentacle. (She has always been the Mistress of the Animals.) Her blessing was given to them, and as Her power flowed through me it was almost tangible.

Working 'The Mill' followed, in two great circles and a number of smaller ones. It was the largest meeting of witches I had ever attended. The witches chanted in unison, 'Break the chain to Shamrock Farms, so that the monkeys will come to no harm!', and throughout the circumambulations, I pointed the sword in the direction of South America, where most of the monkeys are captured.

At the culmination a symbolic chain, wrought by Michael Thorn and held by two witches, was severed by him. I cannot speak for the others, but a great deal of vital *élan* had gone off me, and I was in urgent need of sustenance. The evening continued with an excellent vegetarian buffet, dancing and general jollifications.

The magic that witches perform under the auspices of the Old Gods manifests on the material plane through some form of human intervention, and two days later a report appeared in a Florida newspaper stating that the authorities had barred a crate of wild monkeys from being put aboard a plane bound for Britain. My witch friends were duly impressed, as reports of this nature rarely materialize in the States. But the above example was only the tip of the iceberg. A short time later, eighteen airlines decided to abandon carrying wild monkeys in their cargo, and today the UK has banned the use of wild-caught primates for experiments and vivisection. Working on magical levels also aids the many organizations and animal charities around the world and boosts *their* efforts.

Next on the agenda was a meeting of Craft leaders at

Eileen's covenstead. A very special occasion for us and the first time we had entered the Circle, proper, in the USA. It was also the first time, since meeting these high-ranking initiates, that we were together in the 'Wood between the Worlds'. Each person had worked long and hard to achieve their positions and, as I had been an initiate of Gerald Gardner, they were anxious to see how I conducted a ceremony. Their interest showed that, despite what they had learned, they did not assume they knew everything there was to know about the Craft of the Wise, and this alone marked them as true devotees.

In the States, many coven leaders have a document showing their lineage and going back, in most cases, to Monique Wilson, another High Priestess initiated by Gerald Gardner. These documents also carry pictures of Initiators down the line, and often include one of Monique, herself.

At that meeting there were in-depth discussions on Craft matters, during which everyone learned something, ourselves included. Coven leaders, being involved with their own groups and often living at considerable distances from each other, are unable to communicate with their peers as often as they would wish. It is hard work teaching and instructing others, and it is very important, psychologically, to exchange views with witches in similar positions. Ian and I benefited greatly from the dialogue and enjoyed every minute of it.

When at last our plane lifted into the sky, the comradeship of these Brothers and Sisters of the Craft went with us, and we looked forward to our next, 'Merry Meet!'

11 Towards the Year 2000!

Over the last twenty years, literature on the subject of witch-craft has begun to disclose the secret rites of the Craft itself. What started as a trickle has slowly developed into a torrent. (Some present day witches have said that Gerald Gardner also revealed Craft rituals in *High Magic's Aid*, and it may be so, but it has apparently escaped their notice that this book is a *novel* – a fictional story! The analogy is therefore both inaccurate and unfair.)

To place any system of arcane magical knowledge before the general public, most of whom are ignorant of such matters, is to my mind extremely irresponsible. Most magical systems can be dangerous, *if mishandled*, and this is one of the main reasons for secrecy. To most leaders of the Craft, the protection of the 'unenlightened' is considered to be as important as protecting the magical rites themselves.

There are some serious questions that arise from DIY witchcraft. One of the most important concerns the *blessing* given at initiation and, later, the *passing of the power*, for these are things that cannot be bestowed by a self-initiated witch, however well-meaning. It is this vital link, passed down the ages from man to woman and woman to man, that *empowers* the rite – the initiation – and gives it the necessary sanctity. It is something not quite of the physical world: a mystical quality that is created and brought into being through ordination (in other words, through a *properly consecrated* priest or priestess). Thus transferred, this bene-diction will thereafter be expressed in the demeanour and actions of the recipient, who now has their feet well and truly upon The Path.

In the past, certain writers have divulged the secret rites of occult societies, such as Freemasonry. A case in point is the book, *Darkness Visible* by Walton Hannah, an initiated Freemason. This work revealed the rituals, even to the sacred password. (Hannah's *exposé* was written to prove his contention that there were no secrets in Masonry (there certainly weren't many after his book was published). Its completeness was designed to pre-empt criticism: if he had reproduced the rituals incomplete, it might be insinuated that the book was incomplete in other particulars too. Freemasonry ignored the work and continued as though it did not exist – which, when you think about it, was the only thing it could do in the circumstances.

However, unlike Freemasonry, where initiation is supported by regularly paid fees, the Craft of the Wise has no such conditions. And regarding the Craft, it is just as well that important secrets are never written into the *Book of Shadows*. They are passed *orally*, from mouth to ear within the Circle, but only to the most dedicated witches. And what of the Inner Rites, placed beyond the Third Degree? Apart from myself, there must be other witches who have been entrusted with them, for they could hardly have been confined to Jean's family. You can be sure that they will be guarded more closely than ever now.

Most witches are aware that the reasons for secrecy have nothing to do with a priesthood that views itself as a power structure and/or is intent upon upholding its prestige in the eyes of others. Such priestly responsibility has quite a different effect. The priesthood of the Old Religion is known for perpetuating the sacred trust placed in it, and for instructing those witches who will one day come to make up that very priesthood. There are teachers in every walk of life, but in the Old Religion a much more serious matter is involved: the evolution of the soul.

In order to undermine the Craft's system of Degrees, the question has been posed, 'Who initiated the first witch?' Such a question immediately reveals the enquirer's lack of vision; it is much like asking, 'Which came first, the chicken or the egg?' an equally 'clever' remark. Presuming the question refers strictly to the Craft, the person who initiated the first witch would be the man or woman who did so when the term 'witch' was first coined. Before then, initiations took place within the structure of the Old Religion when neophytes recognized that they were entering its Priesthood. Nothing more or less than that.

There is, however, a more mystical answer to this question. Leland's *The Gospel of the Witches* relates how the goddess Diana gave birth to her daughter Aradia. In this legend Diana speaks to her daughter, thus: "'Tis true indeed that thou a Spirit art, but thou wert born but to become again a mortal – thou must go to earth below, to be a teacher unto women and men who fain would study witchcraft in thy school.' The Goddess continues, 'And thou shalt be *the first of witches known*; and thou shalt be the first of all in the world . . . .'

Diana makes it very clear to Aradia that she, Diana, is 'Queen of Witches all', and 'whatever is asked of the Mother in the Daughter's name, it shall be granted.' So there we have it! An ancient legend of a *feminine* deity, sending her daughter to Earth – a female avatar! Quite clearly the first witch on Earth was Aradia.

In recent times, there have been numerous dissertations on the etymology of the word 'witch'. The solutions have mainly depended upon the writer's prejudice, and in many cases what is explained as a 'source' is often nothing more than a corresponding form. Despite the connotations of evil bestowed upon the word by the ecclesiastical authorities in the Middle Ages, and still echoed in some modern dictionaries, there is evidence to the contrary. Germanic sources give the word 'witch' as belonging to a group of words whose underlying significance means 'set apart as sacred', or 'one having the power thus to make sacred'. These derivations exactly fit the priesthood of the Old Religion!

Before the establishment of Christianity, magic and religion were inseparable and grew from early peoples' spontaneous reactions to the world around them. Since that time, however, a subtle change has taken place through which 'magic' has been condemned, although in the context of Christian religion it has merely changed its name to 'miracle'. (Perhaps this is oversimplifying the issue, though, for magic relies mainly upon the human operator, whereas a miracle is considered to occur through the intervention of God.) The result is that we now have a situation in which magical successes are commonplace, while miracles are very thin on the ground.

Apart from the discovery that it was possible to alter and/or improve existing conditions, I believe the real meaning of what is called 'magic' to be the recognition, within oneself, of the seed of Godhood. This is a revelation that has always been the key to the Mysteries and one that represents the *goal* of the Initiate, as expressed through the symbol of the Crowned Pentagram.

One of the most important tenets of the Old Religion is that of reincarnation: the belief that, for the soul to evolve, it must endure many incarnations upon this Earth. The Degrees, which form the hierarchy of the Craft, are extremely ancient, and were initially instituted so as to fill the aspirant with a desire for spiritual growth and attainment. This secret system, which has permeated witchcraft in many different cultures, reveals that the leaders had knowledge to impart – and, I might add, still do.

A French source of 1731 states that three marks were given to witches on three separate occasions, but that only the older witches were seen to bear all three, and this showed them to be very powerful in the Art. (Another, earlier, reference comes from Portugal and is preserved in the records of the Inquisition. Headed 'Confessions of certain Witches who were burnt in the city of Lisbon, AD 1559', the record asserts: 'No one can be a witch [*bruja*] without going through degrees of *feiticeyra* and *alcoviteyra*'.) When we look at the magical initiations of Tibet, we find that there are many different methods and teachings, but mostly they consist of *three* initiations, or degrees. In fact the Lamaists have three categories of teaching, three of practices and methods and three kinds of initiation: the exoteric, the esoteric and the mystic. Each of these initiations involves its own three processes: the common, the medium and the superior. The Lamaists have many symbols and tools that are reflected in those of the Craft, such as the Cup, the Dagger, the Mirror, and the use of music.

I am indebted to Jim Davies of Toronto for the following

191

information in a similar vein. Drawn from the Isle of Man, it comes from W. Walter Gill's *A Second Manx Scrapbook* (1932). Gill quotes an earlier writer, one Kennish, whose poems, ('published in 1844, but many of them were written a good deal earlier') record that, 'By Old Nick and his "suite", a Maughold witch named Old Kate was given discretion to "Initiate those upon probation, And give each hag her proper station".' Gill continues, 'In a footnote to a passage concerning Old Kate's "candidates", Kennish says they were those witches alluded to as being on probation, ere they were allowed to take high degrees in witchcraft. Kate evidently had charge of the local coven in South Maughold, even if she did not control a wider diocese, and was thus a successor of the celebrated Berrey Dhone.'

Berry Dhone's title in the Craft was 'Queen of the Witches', or 'Queen of the Maughold Witches', and Gill says of her doings in Maughold, 'She is said to have been in the habit of sending the lesser witches, her subordinates, before her to open the side of Barrule, at some spot now forgotten, that she might enter the hill. This scrap of tradition clearly implies a belief that they were an organised body . . . .' Gill also states,

> Certain elements in witchcraft have always recognised themselves as an old religion in survival, and have been treated as such by the discerning . . . It has been perversely misunderstood, and its rites must no longer be called indecent and obscene except between inverted commas. It was, in fact, a joyous form of worship which was persecuted, and its celebrations suppressed, by gloomy spoil-sports in the 16th and 17th centuries.

These extracts give evidence of covens in the Isle of Man long before the time of Gerald Gardner!

So, again, we see in these early writings that the quintessence of initiation lies in the one who *gives* it, when magic and mystery are present, and the 'Gift' or 'Blessing' is *transferred* to the candidate. Legomonism, the passing on of sacred knowledge by way of initiation, is a very ancient thing and, for those with the sense to comprehend it, something to be treasured.

192

We now come to the oath taken at initiation. Has this become a bad joke, like those in a Christmas cracker? How can anyone who has taken such an oath – 'never to reveal the secrets of the Art' – betray it? A witch once said to me, 'You know, Pat, some people are incapable of comprehending the nature of an oath', and this may well be true. The neophyte who stands before the Altar of the God and the Goddess, naked and in a state of grace, should certainly be aware of the seriousness of the situation. At this moment, in the sacred Circle, the soul is taking up The Path for the first time, or continuing its experience from a previous life. Having come to the 'Door without a Key', the soul must surely realize the gravity of its position. It is being given the rare opportunity to begin a new life of discovery. By all that is holy, there must be awareness that here – out of time, in the presence of the Gods and the Keepers of the Mysteries – the Rite which transforms and renews is nothing less than sacred.

The Children of the Goddess have always been special people. They have a duty, nay, a solemn obligation, to uphold the oath of secrecy. In olden times the two extremes of Joy and Terror were present in the Rite, to make quite sure that the candidate understood the serious nature of such a step. Yet in this so-called 'age of equality' respect for anyone or anything is practically non-existent. This is not a good thing. Without respect, especially for oneself, liberation becomes mere escapism, which is something quite different.

Respect for another human being implies that the person is worthy of your trust. Something about them evokes this feeling: you may admire them for their character and/or what they have accomplished in life, or there may even be a wish to emulate them in some way. So it is with Initiation. Something within, desires expression – improvement, dare I say, to be more like the Gods? For this is the goal of the exercise: to progress beyond the need of being embodied. After many lifetimes, it finally dawns upon the individual that there must be something superior to Self – some quest in the spiral of evolution that all of us, in our different ways, are moving towards.

There seems to be much confusion concerning the 'Craft of the Wise', and what is known as paganism. The idea that a person must belong to the Craft in order to worship the Old Gods and celebrate the festivals, is quite absurd. In Britain, alone, there are thousands of people who are pagans. They do not belong to the Craft but, like the people of old, they gather at sacred sites and do their own thing, as they say. These people love the Goddess and the Horned God as much as any witch does, but they are not stupid enough to think they must enter the Craft, or even initiate themselves, in order to acknowledge the Gods of the Old Religion. These young people are the neo-pagans of the Aquarian Age. They devote much of their time to studying ancient crafts and subjects such as herbalism, the runes and the Tarot. They are the people who are in tune with the changing times, and whose children will be born in the New Age.

There are some who say that the Craft must change in order to keep in touch with new concepts arising in the world. I really cannot see why. In ages past there have been untold changes in society (not always beneficial ones), and yet the Craft has existed and continued practising its teachings. This is because its ethos is relevant in *any* Age.

Recently, certain scientists have shown much interest in matters concerning the borderline energies. Such things as telepathy, hypnotism and clairvoyance, which only a few decades ago would have been dismissed out-of-hand as meaningless mumbo-jumbo, are compelling attention and examination. Yet these very things have been recognized and used by witches for hundreds of years! And the ancient idea that plant life grows better with human love and care is now accepted as a valid concept which brings positive results. Yet this act of giving recognition and love to Nature, 'the Mother of All Living', also originated in the Old Religion and is objectified in festivals and folk customs throughout the year.

It is precisely because the Craft is based upon *ancient* values, and has preserved them, that it will be of vital importance in the future. No other magico-religious framework in the Western world is more successful than the Craft of the Wise. It answers the need for spiritual evolution, provides knowledge of the after-life, grants an understanding of Nature's rhythms and tides, and has a host of associated traditions gleaned from a venerable heritage. My advice to 'young' witches is this. By all means *build* upon what you have been taught, but never destroy the foundations.

The Craft of the Wise has seen many esoteric societies crumble and disappear through a variety of human weaknesses. And over the last fifty years (due almost entirely to the efforts of Gerald Gardner) it has emerged from an enforced hibernation and attracted thousands of devotees, most of whom were initially drawn to it because of a desperate need of the Great Goddess.

The blame for many of the world's present ills rests with the Christian Church, which promoted the idea that human beings came from God and therefore have no relationship with the natural world. For centuries, the idea that humanity was alone in an alien and hostile universe has continued to be taught in religious education. This philosophy is anathema to the Old Religion, which has always seen the universe as the 'Dance of Life', where everything exists in harmony and in which humanity is the microcosm of the starry macrocosm. In other words, we are made from the same stuff that made the stars!

Possibly, the most negative doctrine of established religion has been the subordination of women – a natural extension of the concept that God is wholly male. Since the Cycle of the Moon, however, great changes have occurred. (A Cycle is an astrological theory which affirms that the seven major planets nearest the Earth predominate [according to the Chaldean System] in both their Natural and Diurnal orders of sequence, for a fixed period of 36 years. The Sun and the Moon are regarded as planets for the sake of convenience.) The Moon Cycle ran from 1945 to 1981, and in the middle of it, on Sunday, 20 July 1969 at 10.56 p.m. (Florida time), men actually set foot on that feminine orb, and thus established a *physical* link with it. Recognition of the Great Goddess had already begun, and revolutionary changes in society quickly followed. A totally different set of values emerged, with equality for the female being paramount.

Women's Liberation was born, combating what had hitherto been a masculine-oriented world, and this battle is still going on. Patriarchal ideas of marriage and marriage vows began to be challenged by females in an unprecedented manner. The chief question was, why should women be virtually owned by men when they marry, and why should they have to adopt their husband's surname? Ergo, why should they have to lose their identities in this way? Was it to remind them that they came from a man's rib-bone in the first place, and so must be suitably obedient to their lord and master? It is hard to credit that male-dominated belief systems have been able to instil in their followers such fanciful and silly stories, and for such an unconscionable period of time. But it shows why the Great Goddess must continue to grow in strength within Her own particular sphere. The more people acknowledge Her, the stronger will She become.

Only now, in the dying years of the twentieth century, have women penetrated that bastion of male supremacy the Christian Church. – A few years ago this would have been inconceivable. Even so, in certain quarters they are known as 'women priests', a term that still clings to the masculine noun, despite the existence of the appropriate feminine noun *'priestess'* (but this word has associations with the Old Religion and the predominance of women, so it is naturally hateful to the Church).

The word 'priestess' speaks of a time when the female was the presiding officiate in religious ceremonies, and when *feminine* witchcraft, far from being a modern innovation in the States, was the oldest (and the only) form of witchcraft in Europe. Modern, all-women covens are merely going back to ancient roots.

Many churchmen were up in arms when the first women were ordained as 'priests'. In March 1994, under the heading 'Burn 'em Vicar mixes his Bitches with Witches!', the *Daily Mirror* reported the uproar caused by Lincolnshire vicar the Rev. Anthony Kennedy, who said 'Witches should be burned at the stake', and 'If we were living in medieval times I would probably set fire to them myself!' (He was also angry at being misquoted. 'I never said "burn the bloody bitches", that is not a term I use. I said, "Burn the bloody *witches*", and I stand by that.') Another vicar from the Bristol area commented that so-called 'women priests' were nothing more than transvestites, as they were dressing in the male attire of a priest. Since the dictionary definition of 'transvestite' is a 'person seeking

196

sexual pleasure by wearing clothes normally worn by the opposite sex', this is a damning indictment, indeed. However, the robes of the clergy were initially copied from those worn by priestesses in Ancient Egypt!

In order to understand the important issues that lie behind the present social revolution, we must look at the ancient form of divination, the Tarot. Within the 78 cards of a regular deck, lies the sum of Western esoteric wisdom, preserved over a long period of time. The Tarot, itself, precludes time, as we know it, which is why it is able to reveal the 'future' to us.

The Major Arcana portray the human journey through life by means of 22 cards of suitable imagery, in which the soul is represented by 'The Fool' and numbered zero. The 17th Arcanum, The Star, depicts (in most decks) a beautiful naked woman pouring liquid from two urns – into the ground from one, into a stream from the other. Above her in the firmament, a huge star dominates the scene; this is Sirius, a sun in a distant galaxy, many times larger than our own sun and from which, it is held, our star was born.

The Tarot is intertwined with the twelve signs of the Zodiac and the planets of the Solar System, and The Star both expresses the ideals of the sign Aquarius and also reveals the Star Goddess herself, pouring out the essences of regeneration and rebirth in the new Aquarian Age.

An Age is approximately two thousand years, the time it takes for the sun to travel, or appear to travel, through one sign of the Zodiac. This astronomical event, known as the Precession of the Equinoxes, is determined by the position of the sun on the equator at the vernal equinox and by the North Pole's relation to the Pole Star. Energy flows *through* the Earth from the North Pole – the *positive* pole – and at the present time the North Pole points to Polaris, the Pole Star. (Because the Earth wobbles on its axis, millions of years ago the Poles were reversed – the South Pole then being the dominant factor.) The phenomenon is based upon the North Pole's alignment with the Pole Star and affects the *entire* globe.

The Sun, moving backwards through the Zodiac, has recently completed its sojourn in Pisces and is now inching its way into the sign of Aquarius, where it will reside for the next two thousand years. A Great Year is a time-span of 24,000 years , during which the Sun completes its passage through all the twelve signs – a mere breath in galactic terms.

We must not forget the ruler of Aquarius: Uranus, the 'Magician of the Zodiac'. This planet is well-known for causing transformation and change to occur – and very suddenly. Uranus entered Aquarius on 12 January 1996, and I regard this event as the true beginning of the New Age.

One of the most important aspects of Aquarius is that of *extension*, and if we look at Aquarius as the global ruler of the New Age, this aspect points strongly to travelling amongst the stars. Extension will also occur on mind levels, where psychic abilities such as clairvoyance and telepathy will eventually be accepted as the norm, moving towards super-consciousness. The Spiral of Evolution will continue to draw humanity nearer to perfection, and the Craft of the Wise – at the heart of the Old Religion – will have an influential part to play in working with those dedicated to a similar task, wherever that work is needed.

The Great Goddess has been with us from the beginning of time. In the darkness of subterranean caverns she dwelt as Black Isis, and as 'Mother of all Living' she waited at the Gate of the Byre. The Earth Mother was exalted in the great rock-hewn temples raised in her honour, and as Isis, Queen of Heaven, she was adored in the gold and marble shrines of Ancient Egypt. In the Circle of the Wise Ones, too, her presence has endured. Like us, she is ever-becoming, and in the future she will be there to guide us as the Star Goddess! Out there, in the darkness of space, a white hand is even now beckoning the Children of Earth to become Children of the Stars. With all this in mind, a particular section in The Legend of the Moon Goddess acquires a startling realism:

> Pass in silence, Diana, through the darkest night, towards the dawn, when shall emerge Lucifer, wearing the crescent horns of the Moon upon his head. Pass then, O night and lead towards light, and then, O Initiate, pass through from darkness into light. Ye who take but one step on this Path, must continue to the end; for this Path is beyond Life or Death.

198

In writing about the present and future, I have been constantly reminded of the past. On a recent visit to Warwickshire, Ian and I walked round many villages, and looked at early churches for evidence of the Old Religion. We had some surprises. At the top of a steep hill in Warmington stands the church of St Michael. Inside, Ian suddenly said, 'Come over here and see what I've found.' He pointed to a high window facing north, and there, at the top of it, surrounded by a circle, was a large reversed pentagram carved out of the warm-coloured sandstone. Framed in greenish light from trees outside the window, it looked quite spectacular. When we looked at the outside, we could see that this part of the church was very old.

Strolling round a church in the village of Radway, we discovered a tiny grave, half-hidden under a bush, and, what is more, the small headstone was carved with a pentagram inside a circle. It was the grave of Nicholas Butler – born 4 May 1947, died 6 May 1947 – a two-day old mite who had been buried well away from the other graves and given a lonely resting-place. This baby's grave, in what was most probably an unconsecrated part of the churchyard, coupled with the symbol on the headstone, would suggest that the parents of the child may have held allegiance to the Old Religion. The name Nicholas was also interesting, as it is one of the names of the Old God.

Once considered to be the outcasts of humanity, people such as beggars, gypsies and witches were usually buried in unconsecrated ground on the north side of a churchyard. When these churches were raised they often accommodated the followers of the Old Religion. Admitted via the North Door, commonly known as the 'Devil's Door', they would proceed to their own altar (the original one), at the opposite end of the church from the Christian altar – which was placed in the east, the direction from which the new religion came. In the course of time, however, the Church grew in power, and the initial gesture of merging the two religions within one consecrated building, was finally abandoned. North Doors were bricked up or securely locked, never to be opened again.

It is well known that witches have always regarded the north as a place of power. They sensed the streams of magnetic energy which flow from north to south, and no doubt realized that the Earth was an enormous magnet. They witnessed the marvellous displays of the Aurora Borealis, and were familiar with Celtic beliefs such as the 'Spiral Castle of Arianrhod', the spiritual realms behind the North Wind where souls of dead heroes dwell in bliss. Streams which ran from North to South were considered to have special magical powers, and the altars of present-day witches are aligned to face north.

Knowing of our interest in discovering traces of past witches, fellow witches Anna Greenwood and Kim Morgan told us of Ryedale Folk Museum at Hutton-le-Hole, near Pickering which contains magical relics belonging to certain witches who lived in the seventeenth and eighteenth centuries. As we regularly pass through Pickering when travelling to Whitby, it was not long before we were making a detour to Hutton-le-Hole – a delightful village set in the rolling green hills of the North York Moors, and well worth a visit for itself alone. Ian and I made a bee-line for the museum and were soon peering into a glass case containing magical artefacts. There was a beautiful crystal ball and ornate, wrought-iron stand that had belonged to an Emma Todd of Ebberstone, together with lots of items owned by a witch called Peggy Deuell of Hutton-le-Hole. These included dice, a spin-wheel, and a magic book, a nineteenth-century copy of the original.

This book which was fascinating, lay open at a page showing a diagram of forty magical squares, each containing a number of diverse occult symbols and signs. (Forty has always been an important and sacred number in the Craft, and just to see all those intricate and varied squares was a thrill in itself.) There were symbols of the Zodiac and the planets, and others more enigmatic. There were squares with dots, figures and numbers, and above the diagram, in what must have been the handwriting of the owner, were the words, 'Peggy Deuell – Her Horn Magick Book, By which all that shall happen in any life may be forecast!' Obviously the original book had a cover made from horn. This immediately recalled the symbolism of the 'Gate of Horn' and the 'Gate of Ivory' – the former representing true dreams and visions, the latter of false dreams and desires. (Horn and ivory were sometimes incorporated into witches' tools and artefacts because they were once animate substances, and held the life-force of living creatures.)

There were many other magical items in the case: wands, athames, pieces of parchment with spells written upon them, a string of hag-stones with holes through them (a traditional charm of the witch) and a whip, or scourge.

A cutting from the *Yorkshire Post*, pinned above the whip, was headed 'Torture whips found under floorboards', and related how in 1964 more than a dozen whips had been discovered under the floorboards of a cottage in Hutton Rudby, North Yorks. The cottage, built more than 250 years ago, had been empty since 1869, apart from a short occupancy during World War II. The article also stated that the floorboards under which the whips were found had been very securely fastened down with a large number of nails. Whereas originally all the whips had been on view, now just the one was on display, but, unlike the other artefacts, there was nothing to suggest that it or the others had been the property of a witch. It had probably been included by those who wished to give the collection a lurid slant.

To an adherent of the Craft, one item in the case was more intriguing than all the rest. This was a copy of a 'Witch's Garter Book'. The pages shown were filled with the names of witches who had received a garter and the dates upon which they were bestowed. (The copy had been made by a vicar of Kirkbymoorside, and the date of the book was given as 1824.) I had not known of such a book before, but it revealed that in those days the presentation of a garter was of the greatest significance. Even more engrossing, if that were possible, was a hand-written letter from a witch informing the recipient that she had made a special garter for her grand-daughter, and had embroidered it with symbols *befitting the girl's status in the Craft*. This exciting discovery is yet more evidence, if such were needed, of the Craft's continuity and history.

These magical items, so akin to the ones used in the present day, struck a deep chord of empathy. Those past witches had so obviously loved the Craft and the Old Gods, as much as we do today.

Another piece of information in the case read:

> The most famous wiseman or magician in this area was John Wrightson of Stokesley, who lived in the latter part of the eighteenth century. When in his consulting-room, he was dressed in a long robe or gown girded with a noticeable girdle and with a strange-looking head-covering on. In this room was a skull, a globe, various mysterious-looking preparations and also dried herbs.

In the grounds of the museum we discovered a tiny one-room cottage with a model of this magician inside. The tall figure dressed in a dark cloak and a kind of bonnet, was gazing into a cauldron hanging over a fire.

In the museum shop I picked up a book by Mary Williams, entitled, *Witches in old North Yorkshire*. This contained much interesting material, including the names of some 88 witches who once lived in that county – I also found one of my own titles, *Witchcraft in Yorkshire* (1973), included in the bibliography.

It seems to me that, whereas the powers of the witch in olden times were generally employed for people with everyday problems, the perspectives have now changed. There will always be a certain emphasis upon aiding an individual, but it no longer appears so necessary or pertinent for witches to devote their unique powers exclusively to parochial matters.

In the last two hundred years evolutionary changes and technological achievements have shrunk our globe and created a much broader outlook in terms of self-sufficiency and day-to-day requirements. In Britain the National Health Service has taken the place of the wise woman, who could heal the sick and play the part of midwife. The witches of today are in touch with global affairs, and use their magic to alter the disastrous consequences of humanity's greed for wealth, wherever it occurs. Many witches and pagans are deeply concerned with preserving the natural world – our heritage of woods, rivers, seas and mountains – and work actively to save the beauty of our planet. Others concentrate upon the many aspects of cruelty to animals. Covens in different parts of the world hold special meetings for meditation or magic. These are arranged so that everyone works on a particular cause at exactly the same time of day or night.

During the last fifteen years, the Sheffield coven and those affiliated to it, have worked to improve the lives of creatures in distress or misery. The results have encouraged us to continue the work. A group of minds bent upon a single objective is a veritable power-house, but on major issues, success comes only after long and sustained effort, and in giving enough psychic energy to the Gods for the magic to be wrought.

There are many theories about how magic works, and they provoke long and intense dialogue, but in the end, the only thing that matters is that *it does work* – it produces results. In this connection, it is psychologically important for a coven to celebrate its past successes – although it must never rest upon its laurels, and any sign of conceit should be immediately quashed, for this attitude would automatically negate chances of future success. The power is loaned to us by the Gods, and is easily taken away. The tools of the Craft attune the mind to particular types of energy, while we, ourselves, become the working implements of the Higher Powers. Through Their Children, the God and the Goddess can and do achieve positive transformations upon the Earth.

Negative or hostile vibrations in the outside world rarely disturb the atmosphere of the Circle. What follows, however is an exception. A meeting of the Sheffield coven had been arranged for the elevation of one of the members on 15 April 1989. Some of us had heard news of trouble earlier in the day at the 'Sheffield Wednesday' football ground in Hillsborough, and that there had been fatalities. This was distressing news, but there seemed no reason to cancel the meeting, and the witch in question had awaited this day for some months, so the preparations continued.

Soon after the Rite commenced, a presence made itself felt and was recognized as the Guardian of the coven. Once before, the Guardian had warned us that an item was missing from the Altar, so on this occasion I stopped and checked, and, sure enough, one implement had somehow been left in the altar cupboard – despite checking everything several times during the day. There were other silly mistakes – mental blocks and a strong feeling of unease which communicated itself to everyone present. I said, 'I'm sorry, I cannot continue. It feels wrong. There is despair all around us.' I knew that for emotional disturbances such as these to penetrate a properly purified and consecrated Circle, something devastating must have occurred in the outside world, and not too far away.

The Circle was closed, the disappointed witch comforted, and another date set (when the elevation was successfully accomplished). It was not until the following day that we heard of the full-scale disaster which had taken place at Hillsborough. *Ninety-two* people had lost their lives, crushed to death in the stands. I realized all too well why the effects of this awful catastrophe had penetrated the Circle: the souls of all those who had met violent deaths that day would have caused great stress upon the Astral Plane. The emotional shock of souls being suddenly thrust out of their bodies was felt by us while we were 'Between the Worlds' and in touch with Astral levels.

When the World Society for the Protection of Animals' 'Libearty' campaign was instituted in 1992, we decided to reinforce it by means of magic. Devoted to the plight of bears, everywhere, it soon achieved major successes in Greece and saved many 'dancing' bears from a life of misery. (The practice was already illegal in that country, but the police were not enforcing the laws because they did not know what to do with the bears once they had been confiscated.) In 1993 a sanctuary was built in northern Greece, where rescued bears were taken to recover and receive expert medical attention. Some of them have now been released back into the wild, well away from their human predators.

Since then 'Libearty' has moved on, and there is now a sanctuary in Turkey, with attention being given to countries further east. In Turkey 17 'dancing' bears were rescued from a wood where they were chained to trees during the night. The rescuers went in under cover of darkness and anaesthetized the animals with dart-guns before snapping off their nose-rings with pliers and carrying the bears to waiting lorries. The sanctuary received them with resident veterinary surgeons on hand, and the bears awoke to a very different situation. There was clean straw, food and large tanks of water, into which they dived, washing their faces and splashing happily.

Our work, and that of many other covens, has now shifted to an even more difficult task that concerns captive bears in China. These poor creatures are held in cages just large enough for them to lie in, and are 'milked' of the secretions from their gall bladders almost every day. They are unable to move for their entire lives (on farms, this is roughly ten years) and are in constant agony. The mind is almost incapable of comprehending such horror.

In harmony with the Animal Rights people, we aim to give all farm animals their five basic freedoms: freedom from fear and distress; freedom from pain, injury and disease; freedom from hunger and thirst; freedom from discomfort; and freedom to behave naturally. A mammoth task you may think, but nothing is impossible in terms of mind power. Constant dripping will wear away a stone!

Some sections of the Christian Church have taught that animals have no souls – an instruction that has resulted in much cruelty to the animal kingdom. Moreover, it is a belief that remains far from proved. There are numberless cases where, after death, a beloved pet has appeared to its owner(s) in an astral form.

We know that animals have feelings; they can and do show affection, in fact most of the emotions associated with humans. In their breeding patterns they obey the call and compulsion of the Moon, and in the wild they function almost entirely upon levels that align with the Lower Astral Plane. It is obvious, therefore, that they possess astral bodies, and after death the spark of life, or consciousness, returns from whence it came – the Lower Astral, and its appointed place therein. The Craft of the Wise teaches you to have compassion for animals. Is not the Great Goddess 'Mistress of the Animals'?

One thing which drew me to the Old Religion was its acceptance of visions and psychic experiences. Such things receive scant sympathy in orthodoxy and more often than not are considered to be 'of the Devil'. How can any religion (a word meaning a system of belief in a supernatural power or god) wholly condemn the visions of ordinary men and women, as hallucinations? Why are the dead banished to a far-away heaven world, never to return, and why are these souls forbidden to show themselves to their nearest and dearest?

Followers of Christianity had to accept that they possessed no psychic abilities. God had given man five senses, and they were sufficient. So, for hundreds of years, the idea that a sixth sense might be a part of the human condition received nothing but ridicule. However, this important, spiritual attribute has been nourished within esoteric fraternities and is now being recognized by a much wider audience. The Chained Unicorn, the magical symbol of the Moon and all that the Moon represents, is breaking free from its shackles.

I was lucky enough to be blessed with a sense of humour; an invaluable asset in life. It is said that the gods love laughter, and there is never any lack of it in *my* coven. Witches must also learn to laugh at themselves, and towards the end of a meeting it is very important, psychologically, to let one's hair down while sharing the Communal Horn Cup. Laughter is a great leveller.

One incident which caused much hilarity occurred when I learned through the grape-vine that I had a son – or, to be precise, two sons! It appeared that on separate occasions, two young men asserted that they were the offspring of Patricia Crowther! (As it happens, I have never given birth in a *physical* sense, and *I* should know!) There was also the letter from a female in the States who informed me that she had been initiated into the Sheffield coven by Arnold Crowther in 1963 at the age of sixteen! This statement was false, even down to the person's age, as we never initiated anyone under the age of twenty-one. How could she write such balderdash to me? One wonders what she hoped to gain – maybe a certificate to say, 'I told the biggest whopper!' or perhaps she thought my memory was failing due to what must be my considerable age. I remember all the people who entered the Sheffield coven, and I have kept the minutes of every meeting since the coven's inception.

Humour is also important when giving lectures. At some

stage in the proceedings it should be invoked. Laughter helps to relax an audience and breaks down any barriers. For example, I often mention a letter I received from a man who asked me to forward him a lucky charm made of gold, silver, or ivory – and would I send him two, just in case he lost one! And the time when Gerald Gardner received a letter from a clergyman, offering one pound sterling for a tape recording of the witches' secret rites! Gerald remarked, 'Well, you know, even Judas got thirty bob!'

The way in which certain instructions are phrased can be amusing if taken literally. During an evening with the Townswomen's Guild, I happened to enter a kitchen on the premises where the following notice was displayed. 'Re tea-pot washing. Rinse around while in the room and stand upside-down in a clear space. On no account must hot bottoms be placed upon the table!' I found another on a carton of cake mix. 'Each packet will make enough for six persons or twelve small tarts.' A notice in a hotel read: 'Jackets are necessary to eat in the dining-room.' And a sign on a London Underground platform proclaimed: 'Passengers alight at both ends.'

One of the most fulfilling aspects in my life has been entertaining children; I always feel happy when in their company, and it is a real joy to evoke the sound of children's laughter.

I had the good fortune to be blessed with loving parents who gave a shy little girl the opportunity to face the public through the art of Dance. (I had confidence somewhere inside me, it just needed a great big push.) As a result, the theatre was my first love, and the applause and calls of 'encore' from a full house will always be with me. It is, after all, the ultimate accolade for someone with a Leo Ascendant; pay day, or 'when the ghost walks', as artistes call it, was almost an after-thought. I remember with affection all my theatrical friends and colleagues with whom I shared so much fun, and whose camaraderie could be depended upon in any situation. I am proud to have known so many talented people.

Following the Orphic Path – the expression of the spirit through song, music and dance, I was eventually led to the Goddess and chosen to serve Her. This seemed entirely natural to me, if not to some of those around me at the time. Mother was my closest confidante. I did most of the things she would have liked to do (and, given different circumstances, could have done – she was an amazing ballroom dancer). When my mother died I became an orphan. My Brothers and Sisters of the Craft, too, will always be very special to me. These are friends with whom I feel most at home.

I have experienced an exceptionally varied and exciting existence, not least through meeting people from so many dissimilar walks of life, and I must say that Gerald Gardner was one of the most fascinating and lovable of them all. I recall an amusing verse he once sent to me, called *The Awful Curse* –

> May you be cursed while living, damned when dead;
> Your camels die and virtue leave your wife.
> But the Sage who sat beneath the *pee-pul* said,
> Why not wish him *average* human life?

AVE ATQUE VALE!